# FINDING
## SANCTUARY

# FINDING
## SANCTUARY

*Monastic Steps for Everyday Life*

Christopher Jamison

Abbot of Worth

**LITURGICAL PRESS**
Collegeville, Minnesota

www.litpress.org

First published in Great Britain in 2006
by Weidenfeld & Nicolson

© Christopher Jamison 2006

This edition for the United States and the Philippines published by Liturgical Press,
Saint John's Abbey, P.O. Box 7500, Collegeville, Minnesota 56321-7500.
www.litpress.org.

All images © Royalty-Free CORBIS, except:
Hand Turning Door Handle © Claudia Kunin/CORBIS
Boy Reaching for Book © Randy Faris/CORBIS
Climbing the Corporate Ladder © Paul Hardy/CORBIS
Riding the Escalator © Steve Prezant/CORBIS
Road Sign That Says "THE WAY" © Jed & Kaoru Share/CORBIS
Open Door and Chair, Stein Am Rhein, Switzerland © Monte Nagler Photography
The Monastery © Tiger Aspect Productions

| 3 | 4 | 5 | 6 | 7 | 8 |

**Library of Congress Cataloging-in-Publication Data**

Jamison, Christopher.
    Finding sanctuary : monastic steps for everyday life / Christopher Jamison.
        p.    cm.
    Includes bibliographical references.
    ISBN-13: 978-0-8146-3168-3
    ISBN-10: 0-8146-3168-1
    1. Spiritual life—Christianity.    2. Monastic and religious life.    I. Title.

  BV4501.3.J364   2006
  248.4—dc22

                           2006018968

To my brothers, the monks of Worth

and to my predecessors, the abbots of Worth

Abbot Victor Farwell
Abbot Dominic Gaisford
Abbot Stephen Ortiger

# Contents

The monks of Worth with the five men from *The Monastery* television program, first broadcast on BBC Two in May 2005: Tony, Gary, Anthoney, Nick and Peter. At the time the program was filmed Tony was 29, single, living in London and producing trailers for a sex chat line; Gary was 36, single, and a painter and decorator from Cornwall; Anthoney was 32 and worked in a legal publishing company in London; Nick was 37, single, and studying for a PhD in Buddhism at Cambridge University; Peter was married, a retired teacher and published poet who lived in Bristol.

# Prologue

The BBC TV series *The Monastery* involved five very modern men living the monastic life for forty days and forty nights while TV cameras tracked their progress. The sight of monks responding thoughtfully and helpfully to ordinary people's struggles was a surprise to millions of viewers who had presumed that monks were out of touch. Accepting people as they are was assumed to be the preserve of enlightened liberals, not of cloistered monks.

Yet the five men were not only accepted; they were also challenged. They were asked to listen continuously and deeply to themselves, to other people, and to God. Forty days later, this profound listening had reshaped their hearts and minds as it has reshaped the hearts and minds of many generations of monks and nuns. These men left The Monastery more in touch with life than when they had arrived.

The sense that the Christian monastic tradition has something special to offer is growing among contemporary people of all religious beliefs and those with none. To everybody's surprise, *The Monastery* attracted an audience of three million viewers, and was very favorably received by critics and public alike. The Worth Abbey web site received 40,000 visits in the month following the first program, and during that same period hundreds of people signed up to come on retreat at Worth.

The people who came on retreat here have, to some extent, provoked this book. Those with no background in religious faith have been its particular inspiration. They are a new generation of people who have not lapsed from faith but for whom religion is a closed book or, as one put it, "just a good source of jokes." Their honest searching and their willingness to listen to new insights have been encouraging and humbling for us monks. People want to learn from us, and they tell us that our way of life is precious not only for ourselves but for them too. It appears that our founder, St. Benedict, still has lots to say to people today.

Benedict wrote his Rule for monastic living fifteen hundred years ago when he was abbot of Monte Cassino, the monastery that sits atop an inspiring mountain south of Rome. Italy was at that time a country torn apart by barbarian invasion and confusion, so Benedict understood not only the spiritual way but also the barbarian way. The name "Rule of Benedict" often misleads people into thinking that Benedict wrote a book of rules. In fact, he wrote a book of insights about Christian living, with some practical suggestions (rules) about how to put those insights into practice. The insights are still guiding people today, even though many of the rules have been adapted to local conditions, as Benedict asked that they should be.

In every generation, monks and nuns bring together the realities of their day and the wisdom of the Rule in a new fusion born of contemporary experience. This fusion is the energy that enables monasteries to continue to be places of sanctuary today as they have been for centuries. And that sanctuary can be recreated in the hearts of all people of goodwill. If you are looking for sanctuary in your life, then Benedict invites you into that place of peace with the opening words of his Rule: "Listen carefully, child of God, to the master's instructions and attend to them with the ear of your heart."

# Introduction

"Why did you become a monk?" I am asked this question so often, and it's not easy to answer. I imagine it's roughly equivalent to being asked to explain why you married your spouse: the person asking might want to know your views on marriage (why didn't you just live together?); or it could be that they want to know why you married this particular person rather than another; or it might be part of a discussion about your recent divorce. Each situation requires a different answer. Similarly, I have offered various answers for various contexts. But the answer I really want to give is: "I don't know." I do not know why I became a monk, because the reason I joined is not the reason I stayed. I joined thinking I could save the world by being a monk; I stayed because the monastery became the place where I discovered my own need to be saved. Before I could offer sanctuary, I had to find it.

My personal story, like everybody's, has some ordinary and some extraordinary elements. The extraordinary element is that I was born in Australia to Australian parents with no English connections, but following my father's appointment to be managing director of an Australian company based in England, we emigrated to England, along with my three elder brothers, when I was still a baby. The ordinary element is that I was a cradle Catholic, went to a Catholic school run by monks who were both able and kind, and then went on to university pretty uneventfully. While at university, I knew that I did not want to follow in the footsteps of my father and brothers and go into business. Thanks to the ministry of some fine university chaplains, I found myself led to regular meditation and to working with those on the margins of society—in particular, travelers. Through a series of chance encounters I found myself staying at Worth and realizing that the monastic life here contained all the elements of life that animated me, as well as some inspiring monks.

Did Christ call me? Of course. Did He leave me a voice mail? Of course not. If you want to pinpoint a moment when He called me, it was when I was sitting in my college room one night reading the Bible. Age nineteen, I had decided earlier in the year that it was time to read all the gospels on my own, and at that time I was reading Matthew's. I read chapter 10 verses 37-39, which conclude with Jesus saying: "Anyone who finds his life will lose it; anyone who loses his life for my sake will find it." That touched a chord and seemed to me to describe the dilemma I faced: finding everything that a career offered and losing what I valued, or losing what was on immediate offer and finding something else at the hands of God. Seen in those terms, the decision is not difficult; working that decision through in practice and explaining it to everybody else is much harder. So I gave it a go, thinking I would probably not make it past novice; and, to my surprise, I grew into the life more and more.

Throughout this book, the call of Christ is the hidden assumption. I say "hidden" because I won't keep on repeating it; I say "assumption" because the insights of Benedict assume the insights of Christ. The Rule of Benedict is a commentary on the gospel, and it is woven out of quotations from the Bible. This book will help you to enter into the teachings of Benedict, but it will not assume that you, the reader, are Christian. What it will assume, however, is that Benedict and his monastic tradition are Christian. It is certainly true that Christian monks share much in common with our monastic brothers and sisters of other religions, especially Buddhist monks, but a word of caution is needed when talking about these similarities. The monastic life of celibacy and prayer is strikingly similar in the Catholic and Buddhist traditions; it is one of Worth's privileges that we have a very warm friendship with the Buddhist monastery at Chithurst here in West Sussex. We have good dialogues, but we recognize that there are differences as well as similarities between us. We Benedictines are Christian believers, and so to understand us fully requires an understanding of the teachings of Christ.

If your response to God and to Christ is: "I do not know what to believe," then that is fine: just keep an open heart and mind as you read this book. *Finding Sanctuary* is written very much with you in mind, and I offer you a story to illustrate the point. One day some old men came to see Abbot Anthony of Egypt, the most renowned hermit of his day. In the midst of them was Abbot Joseph. Wanting to test them, the old man Anthony suggested a text from the scriptures and, beginning with the youngest, he asked them what it meant. Each gave his opinion as he was able. But to each one the old man said: "You have not understood it." Last of all he said to Abbot Joseph: "How would you explain this saying?" and he replied: "I do not know." Then Abbot Anthony said: "Indeed, Abbot Joseph has found the way, for he has said: 'I do not know.'"

This story is taken from *The Sayings of the Desert Fathers and Mothers,* a collection of ancient wisdom that often shocks us into reconsidering our assumptions about how life works. These fathers and mothers were the first monks and nuns of the Christian tradition, and they lived in the desert areas of the Middle East during the fourth and fifth centuries. The most famous of them was Anthony of Egypt, about whom there are many stories such as the above. Viewed from our perspective today, these monks and nuns inhabit a strange world full of demons and temptations, angels and miracles. Some seem very odd people, who lived in ways that offend modern sensibilities. One of the strangest of all was the Syrian, Simeon Stylites, who lived on top of a column but was considered a saint by those who came to visit him. On reflection, if David Blaine can fast for forty-four days inside a Perspex box hanging over the Thames and have 250,000 fans come to visit him, then maybe the desert fathers were not so peculiar after all! Even in their own day, however, they were considered strange; yet the rich and powerful sought them out for advice. They had left behind the busyness of their day and found a sanctuary that others envied. Their wisdom was and is precious.

Within their desert sanctuary, the fathers and mothers of the desert became some of the first great spiritual teachers and some of the first psychologists; they plumbed the depths of the soul, and from those depths they invited people to look at spirituality in ways that are imaginative and challenging. Benedict was born in 480, just at the end of their heyday, and he revered them as his mentors. They are remarkable guides, combining wit, insight, and wisdom in a mixture that we moderns can only envy. As we go through this book, the sayings of the desert fathers and mothers will accompany us on our journey in search of sanctuary.

Our search involves learning how to build a sanctuary in the midst of everyday life. So, to begin with, I invite you to consider the busyness of modern life and what causes it. Then I ask: what steps can somebody take in order to find sanctuary there? I have chosen seven steps from the monastic tradition and each step leads to the creation of a particular part of the sanctuary: the door, the floor, the walls, the roof, or the windows, not forgetting the furniture and fittings. This sanctuary is built by heart and mind, but it is no less real for that.

The Abbey Church at Worth is a large building, but it is very simple in design and it is always open, day and night. I hope that the sanctuary that you build in your life as you read this book will be as spacious, as beautiful, and as welcoming.

# PART ONE
## *Everyday Life*

# How Did I Get This Busy?

Recipes for busy moms, tips for busy teachers, workshops for busy executives—these are just some of the courses around today that help us cope with being too busy. People speak and act as if being busy is a force beyond their control, as if somewhere back in history a malign spirit of busyness invaded the planet. There was a time, in the good old days, when people had time, and life moved at an easy pace. But modern society changed all that, and now we are stuck with a way of life that is a breathless rush. "People don't have time like they used to"—and we all nod in agreement.

I have recently taken to asking those who come to the monastery on retreat where they find sanctuary in their lives today. Some of them admit frankly that they do not have any sanctuary; they are just too busy, and that is why they have come on retreat. This busyness is so endemic that even the act of coming on retreat for forty-eight hours evokes in them strong feelings of guilt. "I've had to leave my spouse to look after the children," they say, or "I should be working"; and so they feel that simply being in the monastery is self-indulgent. Then I ask them: "Why have you allowed yourself to get into this state?" The question throws them, because until that moment most had assumed that the excessive busyness of their lives was somebody else's fault. They and many others have an unspoken assumption that modern life is busy, that being busy is one of the penalties of living in a developed country in the twenty-first century, and that one day they will make a life decision to escape from all this . . . but not yet.

"Busy" is, of course, a relative term, a fact humorously illustrated by the advertisement that shows a man on a bike stuck behind a stationary but solitary bus on a Caribbean island. The cyclist complains: "Man, this is gridlock!" Leaving aside for the moment the relative nature of being busy, the foundations of our contemporary feeling of "being too busy" are worth a closer look.

Put simply, if somebody says they are too busy, then either they *are* too busy or they *think* they are too busy. Either way, the responsibility lies with them; they choose to lead a busy life, or they choose to think that they do. When I have said to people on retreat that they have chosen to be busy, they find this impossible to accept. Yet the experience of the five men seen in *The Monastery* suggests that this is truer than most people realize. Several of them had great difficulty just accepting that they didn't have much to do and that they had to be silent for long periods. Stillness and silence were truly foreign to them and, at first, not that welcome: Tony and Anthoney in particular kept using their mobile phones for days after their arrival and found it difficult to settle into not being busy. So some explanation is required of the way this choice for busyness is made. In Britain, it is rooted in the way life changed in the eighties, so a quick look at that upheaval may offer a fresh perspective on the pressures that make people so busy in Britain today. Other developed countries could tell similar stories.

Twentieth-century Britain once had a raft of organizations, such as trade unions and professional bodies, that dictated much of the pace of ordinary life. For example, trade unions protected people from working long hours for poor pay and professional associations enabled doctors, lawyers, and other professionals to regulate the way they worked. But by the 1980s British industry was falling behind commercially in the global economy, and it fell to the Thatcher government to tackle the problem. Their solution was to destroy or reduce the power of institutions such as trade unions. This would enable market forces to operate more freely and so force the British economy to modernize; the demands of the market would now dictate every aspect of life. This applied not only to the working classes but to the professional classes as well. Far from protecting people, the state now sought to maximize competition in order to ensure that market forces decided everything in the lives of its citizens. For example, the national institutions that provided water, gas, and electricity were sold off to private companies, which cut costs while trying to meet the demands of the customer in new ways. Even the National Health Service had to create an "internal market."

## "WE'RE ALL CUSTOMERS NOW"

This market economy led inevitably to the emergence of a consumerist approach to life, with the slogan: "Let the customer decide." In this consumerist world, people are offered the promise of purchasing whatever they choose from an ever-expanding range of continuously improving products. In the traditional marketplace the stallholders always sold the same thing in the same way, in the same place and at the same time; but in the modern marketplace everything is bigger and better than the last time, and it's available wherever and whenever you want it. So now, anywhere at any time, you can buy the latest version of everything. While theoretically the consumer can say, "I've had enough," and stop consuming, in fact the market works hard to make sure the consumer never says that.

So British society now defines a person as a consumer. This is neatly illustrated by the transition in announcements on the rail system by which travelers have ceased to be "passengers" and have become "customers" instead. Even schools and hospitals (and not only private ones) now treat pupils and patients as customers. We are all customers now.

Now this consumer-driven outlook is dependent on some hidden assumptions: first, the assumption that there is an infinite supply of goods coming from an infinite production line. The second assumption is that the consumer will have to engage in endless productive work in order to earn the money to fund the endless consumption.

Where the professional classes once led a leisurely life, now they have become stressed out. Where the working man once relied on a job for life in a stable industry, now "he got on his bike and looked for work." We are all in thrall to consumption, both our own consumption and that of the customers who provide our wages. This is the context with which we have chosen to collude, and we are all too busy as a result. In this sense, we *choose* to be too busy.

In simple terms, the consumerist lifestyle forces people to work too hard in order to fulfill their consumer ambitions. The desire for the bigger car or the better vacation drives people to overwork, and those caught up in this cycle have difficult decisions to make about whether to give up some of these ambitions in order to make room for sanctuary. Armed with this understanding, you can stand back from our culture and question it. You are a free person and you can choose how busy you want to be. Freely choosing to resist the urge to busyness is the frame of mind you need before you can take any steps toward finding sanctuary.

## ✦— "GET AWAY FROM IT ALL?" —✦

Much of the modern tourist industry is built on the assumptions I have just outlined. The promise of a respite from being too busy fuels the language of travel brochures: "Want to get away from it all? Take the family to Disney World!" Tourism offers temporary respite from this world of frantic busyness by offering yet another consumer product as the antidote: the package vacation. All the hard work needed to be a consumer now needs an extra consumer product to take away the pain of that work.

The "it all" of "get away from it all" is an assumed world of ceaseless activity to which there is no answer other than to leave it behind for a week or two by going on vacation. Even before the eighties, the hippy movement of the sixties and seventies inadvertently canonized this belief in the inevitability of busyness by inviting us to drop out from society; if dropping out was the only solution, this implied that changing society was impossible. People are assumed to be too busy because they have to run too fast in order to survive in this greedy and aggressive society.

As well as tourism, other industries are springing up around the too busy belief: health spas called "Sanctuary" offering "heaven," radio stations called "Smooth" offering relaxation, and "alternative therapies" that "eliminate all stress." Now these relaxation products are valuable offerings, but they only deal with symptoms.

Alongside these solutions to busyness are answers in a different mode; a response I have had from some people coming here on retreat was: I can't stand having nothing to do, my hobby keeps my hands and mind focused on something other than my own troubles, in fact I *like* to keep busy. These are what one person called a sort of "anti-sanctuary"—an alternative busy place to go to take your mind off things. Pets, sports, hobbies are all busy occupations, each a personally chosen busyness, an antidote to the enforced busyness of the consumerist society. Yet even these can be turned into consumer products designed to make this exhausting society more bearable but in turn creating more exhaustion.

The tourist "get away from it all," the relaxation products, and the pastimes are providing a respite and a refuge from the consumer/producer world of busyness but from *within* that world itself. They provide only temporary solutions because they are not addressing the real issues; like many consumer products they are instant substitutes for the real thing. Instant coffee is a poor substitute for real coffee. For Benedict and the monastic tradition, the real thing is found in quite a different place.

◆——— MONKS AND BEING BUSY ———◆

By now you may well be asking yourself: but what do monks know about the pressures of modern life and how busy people are? My reply is that while our society has in recent years given way collectively to busyness to an unprecedented degree, the temptation to busyness is not a new one. A story told by one of the desert fathers, Abbot Arsenius, illustrates this. Arsenius was a Roman senator in the late fourth century and tutor to the sons of the Emperor Theodosius. Just thirty-four years old, he secretly left Rome and sailed for Egypt—a midlife crisis on a grand scale. But he was not eloping with a new partner to some paradise hideaway. He had gone to Egypt in order to join a community of monks, finally becoming a hermit renowned for his silence and austerity. Among the many stories told of him, the following one relates to our theme.

One day, in his cell, he heard a voice calling to him: "Come and I will show you the works of men." He followed the voice and it led him to a place where an Ethiopian was cutting wood and making a great pile. He struggled to carry the pile but in vain. Instead of taking some off, however, he cut more wood, which he added to the pile. Then once again he tried to carry it and once again he failed. He kept this up for a long time. Then the voice led Arsenius on further, to where a man was drawing water from a lake and putting it into a broken container so that the water ran back into the lake. Going on further still, he saw two men on horseback carrying a beam between them, one beside the other. They were trying to enter the door of a temple; but the beam would not fit crosswise and neither would draw back to let the other go first so that the beam might go in lengthwise. The story concludes with the voice saying: "Let everyone be watchful of his actions lest he labor in vain."

That brief desert tale from a former leader of the superpower of his day is almost chilling in its relevance for us. We are piling high material wealth that we cannot carry and even when we succeed in carrying it, most disconcerting of all, our pride prevents us from delivering it. The men on horseback are excluded from the temple; their pride prevents them from entering the holy place where they might find rest. The fathers and mothers of the desert knew better than we do how being busy producing and consuming can be a substitute for facing the deeper realities of life. Unlike us, they resisted this tendency.

Drawing on this desert tradition, Benedict knew that as abbot he could spend too much time being busy with the wrong things: "Above all, the abbot must not show too great concern for the fleeting and temporal things of this world, neglecting or treating lightly the welfare of those entrusted to him" (Rule of St. Benedict [RB], 2:33). The "above all" is telling: Benedict knew that this was a particular temptation for those in positions of responsibility. Rather than undertake the difficult task of looking into his own soul and the souls of his monks, the temptation for an abbot is simply to keep busy. So monks and lay people alike face the same temptation to busyness. The advantage we monks have is a tradition that acknowledges this danger and provides some remedies for dealing with it.

## WHERE TO BEGIN?

The real antidote to busyness must be sought outside the consumerist world, and Benedict describes that place for us. He was aware of the barbarian world at his gate, and he knew that he had to create a space beyond that world. In recent years my monastic brethren and I have taken to calling that space "sanctuary." Benedict does not use that term himself, but the word does sum up for a modern audience many of Benedict's deepest aspirations. Finding sanctuary leads us from the problem of busyness to a real spirituality that brings peace. The quest for sanctuary resonates deep into the heart of several contemporary dilemmas and at the same time contains within it the solution to these dilemmas.

For those in search of sanctuary, the root meaning of the word itself actually describes where to look. Sanctuary has two meanings: the primary meaning comes from the Latin root word *sanctus,* meaning "holy." So the first meaning is "a sacred space," and deriving from this comes the secondary meaning: "a place of refuge," a place where someone on the run can escape to. Put simply, the vacation packages and the relaxation techniques may provide the secondary meaning of sanctuary: namely, a refuge; but they certainly cannot provide the primary meaning: a sacred space. Indeed, I would go so far as to say that a consumerist place of refuge will always be insecure because it is not rooted in a sacred space. The sacred cannot be manufactured by the consumerist society because the sacred cannot be manufactured. The sacred is a given fact of life. The sacred is found when we recognize it as sacred; the sacred is not found when we recognize it simply as an item we fancy or as a convenient pause for breath. As one woman put it when she had been on retreat at Worth: "I have started to understand that sanctuary is not just time out, a pause in a relentless continuum, but an opportunity to do some intense listening, made oddly unique through the company of others."

In his Prologue to the Rule, Benedict lays down a simple basic marker about finding the sacred sanctuary: "Let us ask the Lord: 'Who will dwell in your tent, O Lord; who will find rest upon your holy mountain?' After this question, brothers, let us listen to what the Lord says in reply, for he shows us the way to his tent. 'One who walks without blemish,' he says, 'and is just in all his dealings, who speaks the truth from his heart and has not practiced deceit with his tongue'" (RB, Prologue:23–6).

The basic starting point for entering sacred sanctuary is the quality of your day-to-day dealings with other people. You cannot mistreat people one moment and then find sanctuary the next. Finding the sacred space begins with the recognition of the sacred in your daily living.

This truism needs to be carefully unpacked by any person who is sincerely seeking sanctuary. It must not be shrugged off with either "Of course," or "I'm interested in peace and quiet, not morals." The peace that Benedict offers is symbolized by the motto of the Benedictine Order: this is the Latin word for peace, *Pax*, surrounded by a crown of thorns. There is no peace without sacrifice and there is no peace without justice. Those simple insights are most commonly applied to peace between nations or races, but they also apply to everybody's ordinary life and social relationships.

In *The Monastery* one of the participants, Tony Burke, reached a crisis point on the thirty-eighth of his forty days. He had taken his stay in the sanctuary of the monastery to heart. His job at that time was making videos to promote a sex chat line, and the thought of returning to his old way of life was worrying him. On his last night he had a profound experience of the presence of God and he knew his life would have to change. Among the several effects of this experience, one was that he gave up his job. He now works for a regular advertising agency and spends time each day in meditation. If you want to find the sacred space in your life, then you must want to "walk without blemish." You will, of course, fail to live without blemish; but failing is quite different from not even trying.

## VIRTUE: THE DOOR TO
## THE SANCTUARY

In this chapter I hope I have opened up a new perspective on the origins of busyness, and on some contemporary solutions that cure the symptoms but not the disease. I want to end it by offering a way into sanctuary, a door through which we can enter sacred space. I have already hinted at it by saying that the way you lead your daily life is a key part of finding sanctuary. At the start of his Rule Benedict offers his monks a reminder that the ordinary decencies of human life are crucial to the spiritual search. The following short extract is a masterly summary of how to pursue human virtue as an essential part of the real spiritual life:

"You are not to act in anger or nurse a grudge. Rid your heart of all deceit. Never give a hollow greeting of peace or turn away when somebody needs your love. Bind yourself to no oath lest it prove false, but speak the truth with heart and tongue" (RB, 4:22–7).

Before we can take a step into the sanctuary, we have to find the doorway and that doorway is virtue. To help you locate this doorway in your own life, I suggest that you take that extract from the Rule and use it as an examination of conscience. One way to do this is to take each sentence and put "I" or "my" into it. So now it reads: "I do not act in anger or nurse a grudge. I rid my heart of all deceit. I never give a hollow greeting of peace and I never turn away when somebody needs my love. I speak the truth with heart and tongue." If this personalized version is hard to say, then keep it before you as both a summons each morning and a checklist each night. Review the moments in which you have been true to those words and rejoice in those moments. Admit to yourself those moments of the day when you have failed to live out this ideal. Gradually, day by day, let the words move from your head to your heart until they start to shape your day and its relationships. The doorway to sanctuary is the doorway to your heart.

Interestingly, this kind of advice about virtue is now being written into codes of practice for businesses: deceit and lies have proved fatally destructive of some of the world's largest companies such as Enron, WorldCom, and Andersen's. Put simply, virtue is necessary in professional life today, and traditional virtues are now being taught to executives. All this is part of the resurgence of virtue as a necessary part of the fabric of society. The signs are everywhere that the leaders of the consumer/producer society are themselves aware of many of this society's corrosive effects. They now see that virtue enables a person to protect and foster all that is best in their lives—both their personal lives and their professional lives. Virtue enables people to work with conviction and for the good of others; it prevents the vices sweeping us away into a busy whirl of chasing corrupt fantasies.

Of course, some business leaders see virtue as just a useful tool for increasing consumer confidence; they are annexing virtue into the consumerist society, making it another producible/consumable product. But what I am proposing is different from that. If we see virtue as simply the right way to live, no matter what the cost, then virtue is sacred. Virtue is the door into the sacred sanctuary because virtue is not a consumer product; it is not just a refuge from our anxieties nor a pause from a busy life; not something we can purchase in order to relieve the symptoms of modern life. Virtue is the recognition of the sacred in daily life. As we open the door of virtue in our personal and working lives, we will open the way into a sanctuary of peace for ourselves and for others. We are enabled to lead a unified life with the same values at home and at work, a life that is transparent and has nothing to hide.

Virtue is not sufficient to create sanctuary but it is a necessary way into it. Benedict is well aware that the doorway of virtue can put people off, so that they never open it and enter. "Do not be daunted immediately by fear and run away from the road that leads to salvation. It is bound to be narrow at the outset" (RB, Prologue:48). Yes indeed, virtue is a narrow door, but the space beyond that door is infinite—the infinite space of real sanctuary. The sanctuary that you purchase as a holiday or as a therapy comes to an end; the myth of endless consumption is just that: a myth. As we enter sanctuary through virtue rather than by buying our way in, we can choose to leave consumption outside the door. By entering through this door, we can concentrate on creating new and sacred places in the large space that lies beyond consumption. Virtue is the true door into the sanctuary of infinite space.

## STEP INSIDE

Having located the doorway, you now need to step into the sanctuary. This is a sanctuary of heart and mind where the normal laws of physics do not apply. You will not discover it all at once because this sanctuary is infinite. So in a moment you will go through the door and take your very first step inside; yet as your foot approaches the floor you will realize that you have to lay down that floor yourself. In the sacred sanctuary God gives you the plan and he shows you how to build it. Nobody can do it for you; each sanctuary is part of the same divine plan and yet each is different, personal to the one who dwells in it. It is unique because the sanctuary dweller is also the sanctuary builder.

So I invite you to go through the door and take your first step inside. The floor under your feet is the material that underlies the whole life of the sanctuary. It comprises something that so many people today say they are craving: silence.

# PART TWO
## *Monastic Steps*

# STEP 1:
# Silence

*There are times when good words are to be left unsaid out of esteem for silence.*

Rule of St. Benedict, 6: "Restraint of Speech"

Acarpet of silence is what we have to create as we take our first step into the sanctuary—a tall order for most people nowadays. So let's consider the place of silence in the busy world of everyday life. To begin with, notice that silence is often considered awkward: witness the embarrassed silence of people at a party not sure what to say next, or of a group of strangers stuck in an elevator. These awkward silences disturb us. On the other hand, there is a silence that consoles us: the silence of a sleeping child, the stillness of mountains, or the tranquillity of a church.

As with silence, so too with sound: there is good sound and bad sound. But in the case of sound we have a separate word to describe the bad sort—namely, noise. Incessant noise creates stress and deprives us of sleep, while at an extreme it can be used as torture; and yet the right kind of sound is highly sought after. Really loud rock music is popular and clubs pump it out to paying customers; it may be noise to some of us, but to others it is "the latest sound." Even in the milder context of a supermarket or an elevator, canned music is present in the background to provide the right kind of sound and to keep bad silence at bay. More positively, classical music is used in classrooms to calm the atmosphere and to help students concentrate. In essence, the wrong kind of noise disturbs us and the right kind of sound helps us.

The challenge for people today is to find positive silence in the city, the setting in which most people now live. Perhaps the biggest challenge, however, is to help people find positive silence inside themselves. In the quest for sanctuary people often find the biggest obstacles are inside themselves. These obstacles are of different kinds and at different levels, but the first one that people most commonly encounter is what we can call "noises inside my head." This is not "the voices inside my head" of the delirious or insane person; this is the simpler phenomenon of thoughts racing in all directions at once.

At Worth we have many people who come on retreat for the first time, and we invite them to spend some time in silence. At one level this is what they crave and why they have come. So they are often shocked to discover that no sooner have they removed the daily routine, set aside the television, and found a place of silence than their head fills up with trivial thoughts: "I wonder what's for supper." "I need to book an appointment with the dentist." "I need to write to my cousin." People discover, to their shame and embarrassment, that the busyness of life has got right inside their heads and they can't get it out. To empty our heads of all thoughts, words, and images is almost impossible; yet somehow these distressing internal noises need to become gentle internal sounds.

◆——     MONASTIC SILENCE     ——◆

To help us address the challenge of "the noises in my head," I
want to look at how we try to avoid silence and then at how
we can choose to build times of silence into our lives. The
five men in *The Monastery* found silence the hardest aspect
of the monastic life to handle and, in some ways, they never
really came to grips with it. In the monastic tradition there
is a basic background of silence: where people today commonly have background music, monks have background
silence. In some monasteries (Trappist ones, for example)
the norm is that the silence is broken only in order to communicate during work or in order to receive guests. In
Benedictine monasteries we have special times of recreation
and conversation, while our work often involves pastoral
activity such as teaching, running retreats, or parish work.
All monasteries promote background silence by having
meals in silence during which a monk reads aloud from a
book and by having the "Greater Silence" from about 9 p.m.
until about 8 a.m., so that the nighttime silence is especially
profound. The monastic routine involves not only this general background silence but also two periods of half an hour,
morning and evening, set aside for meditation.

This degree of physical silence is a great help in fostering
inner silence; Benedict knew this and it motivates his desire
to create exterior silence. But this silence is not an end in
itself; it is there to let inner silence grow in the monk so that

the inner life might flourish. A gardening analogy may help here: if you have not been used to silence, the first things you notice when you enter into it are the distractions inside yourself—the weeds. Even when you pull them up and throw them away, they grow back again quickly and you wonder why you bothered. But you need to keep weeding in order to let the flowers grow. The flowers in this case are the words from God that can grow if you have cleared a space for them. The trouble is that the flowers grow more slowly than the weeds, and so we give up.

To return to the five men in *The Monastery,* they found that being truly silent was something that took time to achieve. Their first instinct was to fill the silence with something: conversation or music were the common ways of drowning out the silence. After ten days, however, they achieved a breakthrough in their understanding: they started to see that the silence was offering them something they now wanted to receive. So in a moment of drama combined with comedy, they spontaneously handed over their mobile phones and their Walkmans. I had purposely not confiscated these items when they had arrived because I wanted them to be free adults who could learn to make new choices. I wanted them to gain a new perspective and to learn for themselves how to use the silence. One of them, Tony, saw that this also extended to reading novels; this too can be a distraction from what the silence offers because it fills our inner world with distraction. So he handed in his novels along with his phone and Walkman. Having said that, some of the most prayerful monks I have known love novels and have learned how to balance out contemplation and fiction; the need to learn a new way of handling silence does not exclude moments of relaxation, but it does see relaxation as distinct from distraction.

◆——      CARTHUSIAN SILENCE      ——◆

In *The Monastery,* Worth was not the only monastery that opened its doors to the television cameras. The monks of the Charterhouse at Parkminster responded generously to our request to allow the five men staying at Worth to visit them, accompanied by the television crew. Such access to a Charterhouse is rare, and the visit made a deep impact both on the men and on the viewers. The reason that I want to talk about the Carthusians in the context of a chapter on silence is that they have the most profound life of silence of any religious order. So, first, a word about their history.

In 1084 St. Bruno led a band of six companions into the wilderness area of the French Alps known as la Chartreuse. They aimed to imitate the way of life of the desert fathers, following especially the example of the hermit monks. They did not follow Benedict's Rule, which is for monks who are living in a community. Instead, they lived as hermits who supported each other and, under the guidance of the Holy Spirit, a way of life evolved that has continued until the present day, a way of life that is handed on not by written word but by example. Gradually, the way of life at la Grande Chartreuse spread elsewhere, and these monasteries were bonded into an order with a rule and general organization. Throughout the world today there are twenty-five monasteries on three continents that follow the way of St. Bruno, the monks being known in English as Carthusians, living in a Charterhouse. Each monk lives in his own small hermitage, including a small garden, with food brought by lay brothers once a day and prayer together in church three times a day. Each monk lives as a hermit in complete silence, broken only by the words of prayer and a community walk once a week. The aim of this life is described as follows: ". . . that we may more ardently seek, the more quickly find, the more perfectly possess God himself in the depths of our souls; thus with the Lord's help, we may be enabled to attain to the perfection of love."

The Carthusian way of life is extraordinary in its intensity, even by the standards of ordinary Christian monasticism. At its heart is the daily life of the monk in his hermitage and silence is the air he breathes. From being an external discipline, it is gradually interiorized, a mystery of an encounter with the Real that surpasses our busy words and concepts. I'll let the Order's statutes speak for themselves on this point: "The fruit that silence brings is known to him who has experienced it. In the early stages of our Carthusian life we may find silence a burden; however, if we are faithful, there will gradually be born within us of our silence something that will draw us on to still greater silence."

There were once twelve Charterhouses in England, all destroyed under Henry VIII. Today the only Charterhouse in the whole of Britain and Ireland is at Cowfold in Sussex. You may be surprised to know that it has a full complement of some twenty monks, with no shortage of novices. The story of the Carthusians past and present reminds us that the power of silence lived in solitude is so real that it can in fact fill all of life for some people. And my belief is not only that it can fill all of life for some people but that it must fill some of life for all people.

## BENEDICT ON SILENCE

Benedict calls his chapter on silence "On Being Taciturn," which means "On restraining the urge to speak." He begins with the words of the Psalm: "I have resolved to keep watch over my ways so that I may not sin with my tongue." The tongue as a source of evil is something that our very communicative era does not consider very often. We think that saying what is on your mind is a good thing; Benedict is not so sure. He quotes the book of Proverbs twice: "In a flood of words you will not avoid sin" (10:19) and "The tongue holds the key to life and death" (18:21), both quoted in the Rule of St. Benedict, 6:4–5. Vulgarity and gossip are particularly frowned upon, especially if they lead to laughter.

Benedict prohibits all the talk that we indulge in "just for a laugh," and this is one of his less appealing injunctions. We will see later on the need for a sense of humor in order to lead a spiritual life, and so for the moment we'll assume that Benedict is not saying humor is bad. What he is saying is that people do talk a lot of rubbish, so in response to this, you should try omitting vulgarity, gossip, and "just for a laugh" from your conversation and see what happens. You may have more time to listen to what matters in other people's lives and your own. The climax of Benedict's teaching is the simple injunction: "The task of the disciple is to be silent and listen."

A Buddhist monk once said to me: "The silence will teach you everything," and this parallels a story of the desert fathers: "A certain brother came to the abbot Moses seeking a word from him. And the old man said to him: 'Go and sit in your cell, and your cell will teach you everything.'" The ability to sit still, in silence, with nothing else except the silence really does frighten many people, and rightly so. Anthony of Egypt explains why: "The one who sits in solitude and quiet has escaped from three wars: hearing, speaking, and seeing; yet against one thing shall he continually battle: that is, his own heart."

When they spend time in solitude and in silence, people inevitably have to wrestle with their own demons. Indeed, that very phrase to "wrestle with one's demons" is derived from the fathers and mothers of the desert tradition. They speak quite literally of the forces of evil that will tempt the solitary monk or nun away from their solitude, away from the silence and away from their prayers. It is easy to mock the personification of those forces as "devils," but anybody who has seriously pursued a life of silence and prayer knows that those forces are powerfully real, whether personified or not. Throughout this book we will look at the dark realities that can surface once silence and prayer are pursued wholeheartedly. The notion that this silence leads to tranquillity is a very modern assumption. The monastic tradition sees any such tranquillity as a short-lived consolation to encourage beginners, which will dissipate once the search for God is pursued with real determination and the demons get to work to prevent any further progress.

This is to jump ahead, however, and we need to turn now to some of the practical questions about how to enable silence to play a bigger role in people's day-to-day experience.

## CHILDREN AND SILENCE

For most people it is a question of finding a time and a place of silence in their busy lives. At this point, the search for sanctuary becomes very practical. As a monk, my life revolves around privileged times and places of silence, but I have also worked with lay people as a teacher and as a retreat leader. So what I offer now comes from discussions over many years with lay people seeking sanctuary.

I begin at the difficult end of the spectrum of busy people: the couple with young children. They have to undertake the task of finding time and space with single-minded determination: if their children are infants, then disruption is inevitable, as life has to revolve around the infants' needs. Yet once the children are beyond the infant stage, I offer a countercultural possibility: train your child to spend time in silence with you. The free rein of self-expression advocated by Dr. Benjamin Spock's famous *Common Sense Book of Baby and Child Care* can be overplayed in family life. The British child psychiatrist Professor John Pearce is on record as saying that child care over the years has gone astray. "I would warn against free expression," he says. "Children need to develop self-control or they become overactive. It's sad when parents are too frightened to set boundaries."

In this regard I have been impressed by families in Latin countries, less influenced by Spock but still very full of love for children, where children are brought up praying with their parents in silence as part of the daily routine. This is also seen in Buddhist countries, where young children spend time with monks learning to sit in the lotus position and learning to meditate. Indeed, Britain's only Buddhist school is a primary school in Sussex, where every day begins with silent meditation for children from age five and up. Within the Christian tradition, Quaker schools also have silence as a regular part of their daily assemblies. Our culture tells us to make sure that our children have physical exercise, and we go to endless trouble to help them play sports from an early age. We could, with courage and determination, do the same for our children's spiritual health by teaching them how to value being still and silent.

## ADULT SILENCE

Of course, parents themselves will have to enjoy silence first, and so now let's look at some adult possibilities. There are two classic moments for enjoying silence: the early morning and nighttime. You can build a time of silence into your morning or night routine. A real help here is to have a physical sanctuary area somewhere in your living space. This need not be elaborate and can be as simple as a candle, a picture, and a favorite text. Or it can be expanded to include a corner of a room with a cushion or a corner of a room with space for all the family. The discipline of going to a place is a real help in finding sanctuary, as is the presence of beautiful objects, either natural or artistic. For a single person or a couple without children, going to this space can be built into a routine relatively easily. It simply requires a deep obedience to the choices you are making about your rhythm of life.

For those with children, the pious custom of having children kneel by their bed for night prayers brings together all of the above points. The child learns to value prayer; the sacred place is kneeling by a bed. This becomes a portable sanctuary—an act of sanctuary wherever you are. If that is not possible for you, then spending time with your children in the family's sanctuary space is a good equivalent.

If you just cannot face this rather organized approach to life at home, there is the possibility of a midday break at work. Many city centers have churches that open for prayer at midday while increasing numbers of companies offer meditation rooms and even on-site yoga classes, free to employees during their lunch break.

Alongside this is the growth of the Quiet Garden movement. This was founded in 1992 by an Anglican priest who wanted to make gardens available to the public, free of charge. Its sites are places of quiet that people enjoy visiting because of their beauty combined with the therapeutic properties of the silence. There are now gardens all around the world ranging from that at Worth Abbey, with its pond, set in the Sussex countryside, to that in Jerusalem, which has a few flowers in a patch of earth surrounded by a crowded city. This movement highlights the natural quality of silence and the growing urge among people around the world to retrieve it as part of their environment.

Perhaps the surest way to help you build silence into your life is to go on retreat for a day or more to experience the possibility of silence in depth. This motivates people to go home and adjust their lifestyle. People today need a strong motivation to break the grip of busyness. Experiencing a retreat can provide the impetus needed to begin the process of escaping from that stranglehold.

To embark on the task of silence building is very difficult to do in a culture that will either offer you a consumerist version ("Come to our hotel for peace and quiet") or consider your efforts to be crazy ("It's not natural for children to be silent"). Whether at morning, noon, or night, however, building silence into your life is a necessary part of finding sanctuary.

## SILENCE: NECESSITY OR SELF-INDULGENCE?

You may well start to feel that this is a rather self-indulgent chapter, as all this solitude and silence is of no help to anybody else; in the end, it's just selfish. This thought is understandable and needs a response. The beginnings of the answer are to be found, as usual, in a story from the desert fathers. As you're probably beginning to realize, there are not many aspects of the spiritual life that they hadn't already thought about fifteen hundred years ago!

There were three earnest men who were friends and became monks. One chose to live out the saying "Blessed are the peacemakers" and worked to reconcile enemies. The second chose to visit the sick. But the third stayed in solitude. Now the first worked among many contentious people and found that he could not appease them all, so eventually he was overcome with exhaustion. He sought out his friend who was caring for the sick, only to find that he too was worn out, depressed, and unable to carry on. The two of them decided to visit their friend who lived in the desert, and they told him all their troubles. When they asked him how he was, the monk was silent for a while and then poured some water into a bowl. "Look at the water," he said, and they saw that it was murky. After a while he said, "Look again and see how clear the water has become." As they looked, the two monks saw their own faces as in a mirror. And the monk said to his friends: "Because of the turbulence of life, the one who lives in the midst of activity does not see his sins. But when he is quiet, especially in solitude, then he sees the real state of things."

This does not mean that the ambition of these men to serve others and to work hard was bad. It is a question of balance. In the monastic tradition, silent solitude is seen as a necessary part of life, not an additional extra. To know yourself and to grow requires the insights that only solitude can provide. Even the most intimate friendship is no substitute for the work that we must all do on our own, the work of silent reflection and prayer.

## HOW LONG?

By now you may be asking yourself how long you have to spend in silence for it to "count" as building silence into your life. When asked that question, I feel like St. Benedict when he was required to legislate how much food monks should eat and drink: "It is therefore with some uneasiness that we specify the amount of food and drink for others" (RB, 40:2). Just as Benedict was uneasy but felt bound to offer some indication of quantity in respect of food and drink, so I uneasily offer advice about how much time to spend in silence.

There is a custom in many religious groups to advise half-hour periods of meditation every morning, and again in the evening if at all possible. This is, in my view, a good place to arrive at, but for most people it is not a good place to start. I suggest beginning with five minutes in the morning and five minutes in the evening; the second period is important, however brief, to set up a rhythm across the day, holding the day framed in silence. You may think that five minutes is not long at all. But if you are going to spend five minutes in real interior silence it may well take you a further five minutes to reach the place of quiet, to get comfortable, and to clear your mind. In other words, five minutes of real silence needs ten minutes in all. Once five minutes of silence is not difficult, you can expand it.

During those five minutes you will need some way of remaining focused. So the final question is: what do I do in the silence? This leads us right back to the beginning of the chapter: what do I do with the noises in my head? How can I be silent internally as well as externally?

For Benedict, distractions inside my head are actually noises inside my heart: they are the result of the natural human condition—the condition of not having a pure heart. Purity of heart is the goal toward which he is leading his monks, and he is wholly realistic about the difficulty of attaining this. To work toward purity of heart, silence is needed; but he knows that it is not enough.

So this first step has led us to lay a carpet of silence in the sanctuary, but it turns out to be an underlay rather than the actual carpet because the opening challenge of the noises in my head still remains. So we need something further on the floor of the sanctuary, something to dampen the unwanted noise even more than the underlay of silence. That further layer is meditation, so the next step is to explore Benedict's teaching on prayer and, in so doing, to lay down the carpet of contemplation.

## Further steps toward silence

*On the web:* www.sacredspace.ie. This popular site offers a new meditation every day, which always includes a "Prayer Guide" with advice on how to be still in mind and body.

*In a book: Silence and Honey Cakes: The Wisdom of the Desert* by Archbishop Rowan Williams is a short introduction to monastic prayer, drawing heavily on the tradition of the desert fathers.

# STEP 2:

# Contemplation

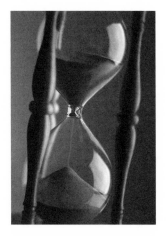

*We must know that God regards our purity of heart and tears of compunction, not our many words. Prayer should therefore be short and pure.*

Rule of St. Benedict, 20: "Reverence in Prayer"

I have never found praying easy, but what gets easier is accepting that fact. So I worry less about technique and more about my fundamental, heartfelt attitude to God while I am praying. In simple faith, I offer myself and my community into the hands of God, with no striving after effect and without worrying too much about the distractions that inevitably come. The result of this is that I find it easier to spend more time in prayer. While time is not the measure of quality in prayer, without giving the time there is ultimately no prayer. Now you will rightly say that a busy parent can pray while helping the children or walking the dog; true, but if that is the only kind of prayer, then I question whether that may not gradually become personal reflection time rather than prayer. So we need to understand what prayer is and is not, and we need to look at some practices that can help us to pray.

During the twentieth century westerners turned increasingly to practices drawn from Asian religions such as Hinduism or Buddhism. The belief grew that eastern religions are more spiritual than Christianity and, as a result, some Asian religious terminology is now better known in Britain than much Christian terminology. For example, the word "guru" is now commonly used in western culture; it is an Asian term for a spiritual teacher, but in the West it now means any kind of expert. For example, "An American transport guru has been hired by London Transport," a newspaper reported recently. So too the word "mantra"; in Asia it means a repeated phrase used in meditation, but in English it is now used as a pejorative way of describing a slogan: "We want better services not just a mantra about improving efficiency," said a group of students. I suspect that the Beatles and their flirtation with the guru Maharishi Mahesh Yogi are partly responsible for introducing these terms into popular western culture.

So in this chapter I want to explore the depths of spirituality found in the Christian tradition, looking afresh at some religious language. I'll do this by looking first at the Christian understanding of two very simple words: "prayer" and "meditation."

Christian prayer is the simple act of addressing God as "you." "We give you thanks, oh Lord . . ." is a common beginning to many Christian prayers. In the Lord's Prayer, we pray: "Hallowed be thy name, thy kingdom come, thy will be done" While this archaic use of "thy" meaning "your" can put people off, nevertheless it preserves an important point: "thou," an old form of "you," can be compared to the French or Spanish use of *tu*, which indicates familiarity with the person addressed. In other words, in prayer, God is spoken to as somebody familiar, such as a parent or friend. To pray is to address God as a familiar friend—to speak to "you" rather than to think about "him."

Beyond this basic insight, the word prayer has two meanings: a general meaning and a specific meaning. The general meaning includes all activity by which people raise their hearts and minds toward God, by which they address the divine "you." The cry to God of a distraught parent or the act of sitting in silence in a church or making the sign of the cross—all these are prayer. While there is usually (but not always) an external expression of prayer, prayer in this general sense is an inner intention and the intention is to communicate with God, to address God personally as "you"; even the simple act of listening in silence is by implication an invitation to the divine "you" to speak. Prayer in this general sense is a quite varied activity and includes acts as different as cries of anguish, total silence, and religious rituals.

Within this general meaning there is a specific meaning, and it is usually identified by the presence of an article "a"—in front of the word: so we speak of "a prayer." In this meaning a prayer is a specific form of words addressing God. Sometimes a prayer has a classic form, for example the Lord's Prayer already quoted; sometimes it can be spontaneous; but it is always a set of words, either spoken aloud or expressed privately.

Putting the two meanings together, we see that prayer can include silence, anguish, and ritual as well as recitation of "a prayer." This leads to an important conclusion: not all prayer involves saying prayers.

Within the Christian monastic tradition monks engage in both kinds of prayer: they say the prayers and they pray in silence. For Christian monks the prayers are chanted extracts from the Bible, especially the Psalms, while the silent time in meditation is prayer within the broader meaning of the term. So the Christian monastic tradition promotes the saying of prayers and prayer. But both are at the service of the great purpose of monastic life and are not aims in themselves. So to understand them fully we must look at this greater purpose.

The great aim of the monastic life for Benedict was as simple as it was demanding: the aim was to pray constantly, in the general sense of keeping the memory of God alive in your heart at every moment of the day and night. As with anyone we love, we enjoy thinking about them and catch ourselves turning toward them spontaneously at odd moments. Another way of expressing this is to say that the purpose of the monastic life is purity of heart, that purity of heart which enables us to see God in everything and hence to be aware of "you" at all times. As the prophet Jeremiah says: "You, O Lord, are in the midst of us and we are called by your name." Monastic life aims to remind us constantly that God is in our midst and sets up a virtuous circle of awareness to help us do this: pray constantly, in order to have a pure heart, in order to see God everywhere, in order to pray constantly.

If you can do this, then you have found sanctuary, no matter where you are physically or indeed mentally. Thus, the mind can be turned to God in the midst of noise and the heart can be turned to God in the midst of complex mental activity, just as a loved one is always present to us. The background of silence, the community prayers six times a day, and the whole organization of the monastery are directed to this goal.

Acknowledging that the regular and communal reciting of prayers is not easily accessible for most people, let's see what else the monastic tradition of prayer can offer. In particular, what help does this tradition offer for silent times on your own, so that they can become for you steps toward finding sanctuary?

## MEDITATION

There is no technique for meditation in the Rule of St. Benedict. Or rather there is nothing that people today would easily recognize as a meditation technique. Now this may come as a surprise, but I hope it is a relief rather than a disappointment. To base a spirituality on a technique for meditation, or a technique for anything, is to reduce what should be a way of life—spiritual living—to a system. Of course, a system fits well with the consumer/producer model: somebody produces a system that people can buy into, sometimes for free, sometimes for money. Benedict has no such saleable system but he does offer meditation in a very non-technical sense, which is why this should be a relief. Nobody in the Benedictine tradition is going to sell you a technique. What Benedict offers is a way of living in which prayer and meditation are key components.

The monastic tradition offers two ways to help us in the silent times: the use of a repeated phrase, and the slow reading of sacred texts. Let's look first at the use of the repeated phrase, something that is not explicitly described by Benedict but was current among monks in his day. Such use was commended strongly by the desert fathers; it was their portable, internal sanctuary. When being still and silent, it kept their distracting thoughts at bay; when they were working, it helped to turn the work into prayer. One favorite phrase of the first monks was: "O God, come to my assistance; O Lord, make haste to help me." This phrase, taken from the Psalms, is the one with which Benedict tells his monks to begin every office (community prayer service). Simple as it is, it can be spoken individually, repeatedly, internally by the monks, and then they sing it communally at the point where they come together to pray.

In solitude, the phrase, or a similar one, can be spoken in time with breathing, rhythmically: "O God come to my assistance" as you breathe in, and "O Lord make haste to help me" as you breathe out. The rhythm of this helps to lift you out of yourself and away from the noises in your head. If those distractions become insistent, one way to handle them is to pause from the phrase, consider the distraction (if it's important, write it down for attention later), and then consciously say to yourself you are putting it aside. If you combine this repeated use of a phrase with the advice on fixing times of silence in your day, then gradually the phrase enters your soul, starts to overflow into your day, and begins to transform your perception of life.

Within the Christian tradition there is also the Jesus Prayer that is so popular in the Orthodox Churches of southeastern Europe and Russia. This prayer involves the constant repetition of the phrase "Lord Jesus Christ, have mercy on me, a sinner," to be said inwardly at all times of the day and night. This way of prayer was popularized by the nineteenth-century story "The Way of the Pilgrim," which describes the quest of a crippled Russian peasant who sets out to say this prayer constantly, not just in his mind but above all in his heart.

The use of the breathing described above is not from Benedict, but is a technique drawn from elsewhere. Other techniques can also help you to prepare the body: sit four square (in the lotus position or on a chair with your limbs uncrossed), keep your neck and back straight, breathe deeply a few times. All these can prepare the body for what is not an art of relaxation but an art of concentration. Imagine you are preparing to hear something very important from somebody important: you would automatically uncross your legs, sit up and concentrate.

In meditation, preparing your mind and body is done not as mental and physical exercise but primarily to allow you to speak to God and finally to let God speak to you. Once I am speaking to the divine "you," then anything can happen, and usually does, so let the conversation flow freely.

Some eastern traditions are very doctrinaire about the use of a repeated phrase. For example, some Hindu gurus (in the correct Asian sense of "teachers") insist on only praying by using a mantra (again, in the correct Asian sense of "a repeated prayer phrase"). The most visible example of this in Europe is the devotees of Hare Krishna, whose repeated chanting and Asian dress have become a familiar sight in our cities. The reason why they chant the phrases "Hare Krishna, Hare Rama" so endlessly is their belief that this constant repetition is the only real prayer. The Krishna Consciousness Movement is, by many criteria, a valid development of much of the Hindu tradition and is in reality more mainstream Asian religion than some of what is offered by suit-wearing teachers who claim to offer the ancient wisdom of the East to gullible westerners. But this insistence on the exclusive use of the mantra as the only real prayer is alien to mainstream Christian monasticism.

Benedict makes no such exclusive claims about how to pray and keeps constantly in mind the aim of purity of heart. "We must know that God regards our purity of heart and tears of compunction, not our many words. Prayer should therefore be short and pure" (RB, 20:3–4). Applying our earlier distinction between "prayer" and "a prayer," Benedict does not see a single prayer or mantra as the whole of prayer. He insists rather on the need for community life and community prayer as the essential framework for promoting prayer in its many forms, the many ways by which diverse individuals come to address God as "you." This freedom of spirit within a framework is something that anybody can replicate in their life: you need a framework for your meditation, but let prayer flow freely within it.

## READING

For Benedict, the principal way to meditate and the main way to be in silence creatively is through reading. In fact, in the Rule, whenever Benedict uses the word "meditate," he is always referring to reading or to the memorization of a text for later use in prayer. For him meditation is always rooted in Scripture.

While Benedict offers no legislation about techniques of meditation, what he does legislate for is meditation through the reading of sacred texts. This reading is his very special contribution to using silent time creatively, and in his monastery the monks did it for up to three hours a day. This monastic way of reading, which he inherited and developed, is so distinctive that we must reappraise the basics of our own modern approach to reading if we are to understand it. If we want to learn from Benedict, we need to reexamine the assumptions that people today have about reading and what constitutes good reading. So I invite you now to look consciously at the activity in which you are currently engaged: reading itself.

As your eye travels across this piece of paper, the printed lines, curves, and dots communicate instant meaning to your mind. Reading is like breathing: you don't normally notice that you are doing it until something goes wrong. So just pause for a moment and notice that you are reading. Weird, isn't it? Now notice that you can make some choices about your reading: you can read quickly or slowly, to extract information from a timetable or to savor the emotion of a love letter. Yet we rarely make conscious choices about our reading: we just go for it, tackling the daily newspaper with vigor or a piece of poetry more thoughtfully.

Most people today are familiar with meditative techniques that can control their breathing in order to increase their well-being. For purposes from transcendental meditation to blood-pressure reduction, gurus and doctors alike recommend breathing control as a good thing. Even popular forms of speech encapsulate it: "Just take a deep breath and relax."

The monastic tradition applies similar processes to our reading. This kind of reading is known in Latin as *lectio divina*. Literally translated this means "divine reading," but it is more accurately expressed by a phrase like "meditative reading." This involves taking a sacred text, usually but not exclusively the Bible, and reading it with the conviction that God is addressing you through this text. Just as prayer involves a person speaking to God as "you," so *lectio divina* involves God speaking to the reader as "you." The connection between *lectio* and prayer is clear: as I let God address me, I feel moved to address God in response. *Lectio divina* leads to prayer and is *the* monastic way into prayer. Before we look in more detail at the processes involved in *lectio,* let's consider the obstacles to prayerful reading that are ingrained in the ways that people read nowadays.

Until the twelfth century Christian Europe saw all reading as the learning of wisdom, whether the text was sacred or secular. In this worldview, God wants to remedy our disordered lives and the ultimate God-given remedy is to learn wisdom. Arts and sciences are to be learned precisely because they are part of wisdom and hence part of the remedy for our souls. There is no separation of sacred learning and secular learning; there is only the learning of wisdom. In this, reading is a holistic activity where sacred and secular are one. To read a text of arts or sciences is to be engaged in the work of your salvation, not in the acquiring of information.

Those who founded the universities in the thirteenth century began a process which led to a different aim: they began to seek information about the world, and to analyze it. This analytic approach dissected the world and reading followed suit; reading was for understanding and controlling life, not for receiving wisdom. Sacred and secular separated and only religious reading was considered sacred. So reading became the very functional activity that it is today: reading for distraction in magazines and pulp novels; reading for information via newspapers and encyclopedias; reading for education in textbooks. Finally, there is reading as an experience of art, as in reading poetry or great literature, this last being the nearest we get to reading for wisdom.

Most recently the emphasis has shifted toward speed; nowadays it is a case of the faster the better: speed reading is virtuous and slow readers require remedial help. So for most people reading is either functional or entertaining and, above all, rapid; rarely do people read with a sense of the text as a spiritual means of acquiring wisdom. But just as the monasteries preserved ancient texts from the barbarian hordes during the Dark Ages, so they have preserved the tradition of meditative reading in modern times.

## LECTIO DIVINA

Before looking at how to do *lectio,* let's look at the question of choosing a text. The monastic tradition favors using the Bible for *lectio,* and there are various reading schemes offered to help you read a Bible extract each day. Some offer the readings appointed to be read in church that day while others offer texts specifically for private daily reading. Alternatively, you can just start with a gospel and read it section by section. I advise starting with Mark's gospel, the most vivid and urgent account of the life of Christ, full of extraordinary miracles at the beginning; don't ask how they happened, just let them interrogate you about what God wants to say and do in your life now.

Other texts are also possible: collections of sermons, serious poetry, lives of the saints—whatever text helps you to read slowly and to hear God speaking. The monastic tradition commends particularly the writings of the great saints, from the ancient texts of Augustine of Hippo through to the modern writings of Mother Teresa of Calcutta. The men in *The Monastery* found it easier to start with such spiritual books for their daily half-hour of *lectio* rather than Scripture, but not everything in the religious sections of bookshops is helpful. So with a text in hand, now is the moment to look at the three key features that taken together make *lectio divina* a distinctive approach to reading.

First of all, the text is seen as a gift to be received, not a problem to be dissected. The first task to which the tradition invites the modern reader is: avoid imposing your questions and let the text question you. Humility is the key to this wisdom. The Australian monk Father Michael Casey sums this up well. "*Lectio divina* is not only a means of discovering something about God; it also helps us to understand our hidden selves. It is not the alienating absorption of a message that is foreign or even hostile to our deepest aspirations; it is the surprising conclusion that our most authentic level of being is mirrored in the scriptures." Let the text come to you.

Second, the *lectio* tradition teaches us that in order to receive what a text has to offer we must read slowly. This brings to mind the recent "slow food" movement in Italy, where villages guarantee to visitors that there are no "fast food" outlets and that all can enjoy their meals in peace. As an antidote to speed reading we need to foster slow reading. Michael Casey again: "Repetition is the soul of genuine *lectio*. It is a right brain activity; we do not grasp the entire content immediately but in a circular manner. We read and advance, then we go back and read again. With each repetition, something new may strike us."

Finally, *lectio* is a way of prayer. Before reading, pray that God will speak to you through this text. During reading, allow the reading to evolve into meditation and then into prayer, and finally contemplation. When the reading is concluded, keep some phrase in mind and repeat it throughout the day so that prayerful reading becomes prayerful living. By this means, *lectio* becomes not so much a technique as a way of life: the text reframes daily life and daily life flows into the text.

The way of life that *lectio* fosters cannot be systematized, but the set moment of prayerful reading can be understood as involving certain movements of heart and mind. As reading for wisdom began to decline in the twelfth century, in that same century a monk felt the need to classify the movements involved in *lectio divina*. It is the Carthusian monk Guigo, the Prior of the Grande Chartreuse, who writes the first systematic treatise on *lectio*. He describes the four movements of the process as: reading, meditation, prayer, and contemplation. By meditation he means a deep entry into the meaning of the text. By prayer he means the reader's response to God in the light of this meaning and by contemplation he means a simple resting in the presence of God, without the need for any further words. He uses the image of eating to illustrate these different stages in "digesting" a text: "Reading, as it were, puts the food into the mouth; meditation chews it and breaks it up; prayer extracts its flavor; contemplation is the sweetness itself which gladdens and refreshes." The image of eating is a helpful one: I am allowing the Word of God into the very fabric of my life and delighting in its presence. In the same way that consuming the bread and wine in the Eucharist is a communion with Christ, so reading becomes communion and begins to transform life. Reading moves beyond information and becomes transformation.

You may be wondering whether such an approach to Scripture is only for monks, so I offer you this thought from St. John Chrysostom, the great fourth-century Archbishop of Constantinople. "'I am not,' you will say, 'one of the monks, but I have both a wife and children, and the care of a household.' This is what has ruined everything, your thinking that the reading of Scripture is for monks only, when you need it more than they do. Those who are placed in the world, and who receive wounds every day, have the most need of medicine."

# ACTION AND CONTEMPLATION

Meditation on a sacred text or meditation using a repeated phrase—both offer us a new context: it is the carpet that we lie upon in order to find rest for our souls wounded by the busy world. We know today that the key to health lies in basic lifestyle choices: exercising, not smoking, etc. The same is true of spiritual well-being. Your basic context is the key, and meditation or *lectio divina* can provide such a new context. You will move your life from one context—the busy rushing from one thing to the next—to a new context that slows you down and enables you to see what is really happening in your life and the world around you. You will still be busy in the sense of working hard, having obligations to fulfill, and going shopping. But you will gradually learn how to keep focused on the essential in the midst of these activities.

There may be a few "highs" in the times of silence and prayer, but they are not the acid test of spiritual authenticity. The moment you think you are praying well, you are in trouble—a theme we will return to in the chapter on humility (Step 4). The authenticity of your times of meditation will be tested in your daily living: in your patience, your sensitivity to others, and your readiness to live with integrity. With perseverance in prayer, what you hear in the silence can eventually be heard in the midst of noise. You will then find sanctuary not only in the times of silence but also in the midst of daily life. The spiritual life is a response to the voice of God lived out in everyday life.

This chapter is called "Contemplation," but so far we have concentrated on meditation. Sometimes the words meditation and contemplation are used to mean the same thing, namely, the self-conscious use of certain techniques to raise heart and mind to God. While this is a valid way to describe meditation, contemplation has a different meaning. It can be described as the fruit of meditation, as we saw in Guigo's description of the movements of the soul in *lectio divina*. One of the greatest Christian teachers of prayer is the sixteenth-century Spanish nun Teresa of Avila. She uses an appealing image to illustrate the distinctive stages of prayer: she describes the soul as a garden, where the presence of God is the water that the garden needs so as to flourish. The water comes to the garden in four different ways: drawn from a well, by a water-wheel, from a spring, and by heavy rain. Each method is progressively less laborious and more fertile. The rain is "when the Lord waters it himself without any labor of ours; and this is an incomparably better method than all the rest." She goes on to explain each method of "watering" as a different kind of prayer. The first three are all forms of meditation, which require some effort by us, but the last is contemplation, when God alone is at work and we are the passive receivers of his presence. The aim of meditation is to be ready to receive what God is offering us, and to some people he may offer contemplation. Meditation is our work; contemplation is God's work. Interestingly, the presence of the gift of contemplation does not make somebody a saint, maintains Teresa. She insists that the response of the contemplative in their daily life is the key to their sanctity and she famously coined the phrase "God among the pots and pans" to indicate the very earthy nature of where she thought holiness lay. Her model is meditation leading to contemplation leading to a generous spirit in daily life; that is the truly contemplative life for Teresa.

This view of the spiritual life and of how to find sanctuary is by no means universally accepted. As we will see in the chapter on spirituality (Step 6), some movements of spirituality offer relaxation and promise tranquillity, themes wholly absent from the Christian monastic tradition. The contemplative tradition of monasticism offers the demanding work of constant prayer and promises the Word of God.

This is the carpet of prayer that we have now laid in the sanctuary. It is not a luxury carpet, however, and it can sometimes have a rough feel to it. The temptation to get up and look for something more comfortable is very real. So we need something to help us maintain our devotion. How can an unreliable human being like me remain faithful? Benedict's answer is by obedience. Therefore our next step in the search for sanctuary is to consider our need for obedience if we are to find true sanctuary and to face head-on the modern insistence on personal freedom, which at first sight seems to be at odds with the very notion of obedience.

## Further steps toward contemplation

*On page 175:* an example of *lectio divina,* based on the parable of the Prodigal Son.

*On the web:* www.centeringprayer.com. This site is inspired by Thomas Keating, an American Trappist monk who has helped many people to discover contemplative prayer.

*In a book: Reading with God: Lectio Divina* is a good introduction to *lectio divina* written by David Foster, an English Benedictine monk.

# Obedience

*Earnestly competing in obedience to one another, no one is to pursue what he judges better for himself but instead what he judges better for someone else.*

Rule of St. Benedict, 72: "The Good Zeal of Monks"

The mothers and fathers of the desert were as clear as Benedict about the centrality of obedience in the truly spiritual life. The story is told of four monks who came to see the great Abba Pambo. Each spoke about the virtue of one of the others. The first fasted a great deal; the second was poor; the third had acquired great charity; and they said of the fourth that he had lived for twenty-two years in obedience to an old man. Abba Pambo said to them, "I tell you, the virtue of this last one is the greatest. Each of the others has obtained the virtue he wished to acquire, but the last one, restraining his own will, does the will of another." The monk who "lived in obedience to an old man" was devoted to the loving service of another. This story illustrates the deep connection between love and obedience in the monastic tradition and, indeed, in life. Today more than ever many careers are devoted to the service of an elderly or disabled relative at home. That is what the monastic tradition understands as obedience. Yet to contemporary ears this all sounds strange: for modern people, love goes not with obedience but with freedom.

◆——— "IT'S MY LIFE, ISN'T IT?" ———◆

Freedom of choice is a core value of modern life. Somebody might express it as follows: "I don't want to be told what to do. I want to be free to be me. I express my freedom by exercising my right to choose my clothes, my job, and my sexual activity." Yet for many people, their supposedly free choices are driven by obedience to a hidden agenda. Take clothes for example. People today are convinced they are choosing their clothes from endless possibilities, ranging from grunge jeans to smart suits. Yet their choices are usually responses to other people's ideas about what they should wear. The fashion houses decide this season's look, the stores mass-produce that look, while photos of fashion icons and advertisements influence us to buy that look. Not many people dress so independently that they can claim to be really free in their choices. Indeed, the whole phenomenon of fashion in clothes has led to the term "fashionista" to describe those people who dictate fashion. Some of the clearer examples of clothes dictatorship are seen among the young: even the very young must have the right style or brand of sneakers to wear, while secondary school students often express not so much individuality as group identity by the way they dress. In those schools where there is no uniform, a powerful youth dress code often operates unwritten rules among the students—rules that students are often too frightened to disobey. So the way a modern person's life plays out in reality is often different from their stated aim of choosing freely.

When people use the language of freedom but live in thrall to hidden rules, they place themselves in a dangerous position. There is nothing wrong with obeying good rules and there is nothing wrong with exercising free choice. The danger lies in claiming to be doing the one while actually doing the other. When people claim to be obeying rules but break them, we call this hypocrisy, a charge frequently leveled at religious people. When people claim to be free but are in fact obeying unstated rules, we don't have a word for it. There is no word for it because it's a very modern occurrence and one that people are slow to recognize. This unnamed feature of modern life is dangerous because people do not know that they are in thrall to other people's agendas and hence do not see the need to escape from them. Apparent consumer freedom can blind people to their deeper dependency.

By contrast with the modern emphasis on freedom of choice, the monastic tradition sees obedience as central to the good life. I say "by contrast" because, if asked, most people today would probably say that obedience is the diametric opposite of freedom. Yet, while they are clearly different, freedom and obedience may not be as opposed to one another as you might at first think.

This apparent conflict between freedom and obedience was once played out in front of me in an unusual way in the 1980s. A *Daily Express* journalist was staying at Worth in order to write a feature article about monastic life. The journalist was interviewing Father Oliver, a monk in his seventies who had entered the novitiate at age eighteen. The journalist asked him: "Don't you think you've missed out on life by becoming a monk so early and having to obey all the monastic rules for over fifty years?" Father Oliver responded quickly with half a smile and half a growl: "Look here, I've woken up every day of every one of those years and freely chosen to be a monk." The clash of monastic and secular cultures has rarely been encapsulated so succinctly. The feature article was never published, but there was an unforeseen sequel to the story. A year later the journalist was in the hospital, seriously ill and near death. He recovered and wrote to us a moving account of his illness and his thoughts. "As I lay close to death," he wrote, "all I could think about was you monks in church, praying every morning and every evening. That gave me courage and somehow your praying saved me." In this story, where does freedom lie?

 LISTENING

So let's examine more closely the relationship between freedom and obedience. The monastic tradition believes that obedience is potentially the greatest expression of human freedom. I say "potentially" because obeying freely involves meeting two criteria. As I said before, obeying something unknowingly is not free choice. So the first criterion for a good obedience is that I must know what I am choosing to obey. Second, I must choose those things that open up future possibilities, not those things that enslave me. So to take an example: somebody who smokes as a teenager in order to be one of the crowd is not

75

obeying freely. First, they think they are freely choosing to smoke and do not recognize that they are simply obeying the crowd. Second, future impaired health is seriously restricting their future, which means that they are restricting their freedom.

So how can people find ways of knowingly choosing those things that will increase their future freedom? Benedict's answer is as simple as it is demanding: listen. That is the opening word of his Rule and it underlies everything that he says. For Benedict, the monastic sanctuary is a place of listening, a place where people listen to each other and to God. So I want to reflect further on the connection between listening, obeying, and freedom.

As with the word "sanctuary," so the origin of the word "obedience" contains an insight into its meaning. "Obedience" derives from the Latin word *oboedire,* which means not only "to obey" but also "to listen." The prefix *ob-* means "in the direction of," added to *audire,* "to hear," which becomes *oboedire.* So obedience conjures up an image of leaning toward somebody, straining to hear what they are saying. "To listen to somebody else" is both the original meaning of "obedience" and a good working definition.

The monastic way invites people to listen, and then choose what voices to follow. This is a double exercise of freedom: the freedom of discernment and the freedom of choosing to follow what has been discerned. Obedience that is blind does not exercise discernment and simply follows the most assertive voice or the voice of the one to whom life has been surrendered. An example of blind obedience would be the handing over of my life to another in a cult, which then disallows me any further exercise of judgement. The fact that we have the phrase "blind obedience" shows that ordinary obedience is not blind like this; it is discerning. This discerning obedience is what I call "obedient freedom."

## OBEDIENT FREEDOM

Obedient freedom is what the monastic way invites you to experience. Benedict is clear that obedience is not just about doing what the boss says; it is about mutual love. "Obedience is a blessing to be shown by all, not only to the abbot but also to one another as brothers, since we know that it is by this obedience that we go to God" (RB, 71:1). This means that you have to listen to other people and not just to yourself. "No one is to pursue what he judges better for himself but instead what he judges better for someone else. To their fellow monks they show the pure love of brothers; to God, loving fear" (RB, 72:7). This is from Benedict's chapter where he describes "the good zeal that monks should have for one another." This is the highest form of obedience, and at its heart is a free exercise of judgement: ". . . what he judges . . ." is the repeated phrase. The purpose of it is to show love, "earnestly competing in obedience to one another" (RB, 72:6). To obey in this interpersonal way requires great inner freedom: the ability to judge what you desire and what the other desires, then to choose freely to set aside your desires for the sake of the other.

In essence, what Benedict is describing is the exercise of conscience. Conscience is not the same as feeling; conscience is the inner process that enables you to listen to voices beyond your own feelings and desires. It is the process by which you freely choose which desires to follow and which to ignore. For example, you may feel free to indulge in yet another beer, but a more discerning attitude will lead to a conscientious choice to stay sober. This may be to obey the drunk driving laws or because you don't want to get thrown out of the bar or in order to have a clear head in the morning. Each of these is a freely chosen obedience, a conscientious choice. To take a deeper example, after many years of marriage, a married person might fall in love with somebody other than their spouse. Feeling might urge them to leave home for the new person, but conscience might tell them to stay. Conscience notices the wider world of other people's feelings, the vows made to a spouse, the law of the land. You can obey your feelings, you can obey your conscience, but they are not the same. Your feelings will be one of the factors that conscience considers and you ignore them at your peril, but they are not the only factor. To follow feelings blindly is as dangerous as blind obedience to anything else. Blind rage, blind fear, and blind lust:

the intensity of such feelings only makes them more likely to mislead people into actions that will be regretted later. Intense feeling is not the same as conscience. The monastic way urges the conscientious exercise of choice leading to obedient freedom.

The belief that you are free and in control if you follow your feelings is widespread, and the monastic way challenges that belief. The monastic way urges free and conscientious obedience, but this raises the question: obedient to what? So let's now examine some of the issues surrounding that question, beginning with a look at the issue of control.

## WHO'S IN CONTROL?

People are understandably concerned to keep control of their lives. One of the features of the improved standard of living in western society is that people own more and are less dependent on the wishes of others for their well-being. This sense of people controlling their own life is not straightforward, however, as urban society is a complex network of private individuals who nevertheless rub up against each other the whole time. One of the ways in which people protect themselves from this inevitable enforced contact, and to help them survive the complexity of day-to-day life, is by putting on various masks: one for the subway, one for work, one for friends, one for the soccer team. This wearing of multiple masks is the way people maintain privacy and stay in control, choosing which one to wear and when to wear it.

The existence of these masks was neatly illustrated for me one day when I was traveling on the London Underground. A girl about age eleven boarded the crowded train with her parents, and her physical features suggested that she had Down's syndrome. There was enough room for her to move around the train, and as she did so she tugged at the sleeves of the strap-hanging commuters and said very loudly: "Are you happy? I'm happy. Are you happy?" Nobody was prepared to own up to being happy and some even ignored her, studiously burying themselves in their newspapers. I laughed and she laughed, and her parents laughed, but somehow not many other people seemed able to appreciate that dropping the anonymous mask of the commuter at this point might be freeing and fun. They remained "commuters," and seemed to fear becoming humans alongside the vulnerable girl. They were intent on keeping up their masks and staying in control. They were definitely not happy!

Masks are, however, more than just ways of remaining anonymous on the subway; they become a whole way of life. One very honest young man recently spoke to me about his experience as a twenty-five-year-old urban man. He described his situation as follows. The young alpha male needs to appear in control and invulnerable, so he does not share his vulnerability with others; he fears letting people see into his soul and his psyche. He fears that they will mock his deep anxieties, his lack of confidence, and his sense of inadequacy. He worries that one day his weakness will be revealed for all to see and that will be the end of him socially. On the other hand, the young alpha male happily shares his body in sexual activity with far fewer qualms than if asked to bare his soul. He feels that psychic invulnerability combined with sexual availability gives him the kind of control he wants in life.

◆——— BEING TRUE TO MYSELF ———◆

From the encounters I have had with visitors to Worth I sense a growing awareness that there is more to life than the mask-wearing, role-playing, sexual posing that sophisticated modern life seems to demand. They speak about looking for new and deeper opportunities to express themselves. "I want to be true to myself" is a common cry among those who are looking for real personal freedom. The desire to be true to oneself is both an ancient and a modern desire. The modern meaning involves the desire to become "the real me." The hidden assumption here is that the visible, day-to-day me is something other than "the real me." At a deeper level, people imply that this other something or somebody is running their lives. Somehow, "the real me" is not able to get out and is not able to take control of life. One modern term for this feeling is "alienation": people feel alienated from themselves; they are living lives that are not the lives they want to live; yet they cannot escape. Put simply, they are disaffected with life itself.

A powerful question to ask at this point is: who sets your agenda? Who sets your agenda minute by minute, from day to day? Who sets your agenda in the long run? Many people would answer: "Other people set my agenda at work and at home; my agenda is set by the demands of the boss at work and of either a partner or a family at home." Women in particular have traditionally felt this burden of other people's agendas running their lives, in terms of housework and looking after children. The women's movement has sought to enable women to take control of their own agendas, but this feeling is by no means confined to women.

Much of this relates back to where this book began—with the sense that many people have of somebody else being responsible for the excessive busyness of their lives. Alongside the busyness goes the sense of alienation. In response to that sense of overwhelming busyness, I have suggested that people take hold of their own agendas so that they can begin to build a sanctuary as an integral part of their lives. I have described a sanctuary where virtue is the door, with silence and meditation as the floor-covering to dampen the noise. This noise needs to be dampened so that people can listen to voices other than their own. The step of obedience described in this chapter involves constructing the sanctuary walls—walls that simultaneously restrain our selfish voices and amplify the voice of God. In this whole process, the true self begins to be revealed.

# THOMAS MERTON

To help this process of self-discovery, I want to turn to a modern "desert father." He is a man whose monastic wisdom captured the imagination of the twentieth century as much as that of the ancient fathers of the desert appealed to the fourth century. His name is Thomas Louis Merton and his autobiography, together with his many other books, became a best seller. First, a little background information about his life. Born in France in 1915, he returned to his mother's family home in the U.S. to escape the First World War. After his mother's death he attended school and university in England and in 1935 returned to the U.S. to attend Columbia University. Merton came from a Protestant family of no particular religious fervor, but in 1938 he experienced a profound religious conversion and became a Catholic. In the year that America entered the Second World War— 1941—he entered the monastery of Gethsemani, Kentucky, where he lived for the rest of his life. Among the strictest and most enclosed monasteries in the Catholic Church, Gethsemani belongs to the Order of Cistercians of the Strict Observance, popularly known as the Trappists. Merton died in Bangkok in 1968 while on a journey around the Far East that involved meeting many Buddhist and Hindu religious leaders. The Dalai Lama called him "an American lama," an accolade that is, perhaps, the modern equivalent of being recognized as a desert father for our times.

Merton's life was a search—a search for how to be true to God and for how to be true to himself. For Merton, these two searches were one search. In 1948 he published *Seeds of Contemplation,* a prophetic book that nearly sixty years ago outlined many of the challenges and many of the responses that are dealt with in this book. One of the key themes of the book is the search for true self. In a chapter entitled "Integrity" he writes: "Many poets are not poets for the same reason that many religious men are not saints: they never succeed in being themselves. They never get round to being the particular poet or the particular monk that they are intended to be by God." People fail to be themselves because it is easier to be somebody else and because they can copy somebody else's success rather than risk their own failure. Working hard to copy somebody else is in the end not selfless; it is, in fact, selfish. "There can be an intense egoism in following everybody else. People are in a hurry to magnify themselves by imitating what is popular—and too lazy to think of anything better."

He notices how the busyness and the false self go together: "Hurry ruins saints as well as artists. They want quick success and they are in such haste to get it that they cannot take time to be true to themselves. And when the madness is upon them they argue that their very haste is a species of integrity."

In essence, he accuses much that passes for being true to oneself as mere imitation of other people's experiences.

The real task of being true to oneself is a slow and profound work; it is not a fixed way but involves search and change. And in the end, being true to oneself can only be achieved by listening to God. Keeping busy is a way of avoiding being true to oneself, so the desire to stop being busy has met the desire to be true to oneself. Let that sink in for a moment and then step further into the sanctuary.

We are now at the heart of this book, at the very heart of the monastic steps into the sanctuary. Here, Merton offers an insight, which illuminates the whole sacred space that is opening up in front of us and sets an agenda for life: "In order to become myself I must cease to be what I always thought I wanted to be."

◆——— THE INNER SANCTUARY ———◆

If your life is centered on yourself, on your own desires and ambitions, then asserting those desires and ambitions is the way you try to be true to yourself. So self-assertion becomes the only way of self-expression. If you simply assert your own desires, you may have the illusion of being true to yourself. But in fact all your efforts to make yourself more real and more yourself have the opposite effect: they create a more and more false self. This self-assertion is false because it cuts you off from other people. If your own desires are your guide in life then you end up imposing yourself on other people and then you start demanding their affection, which can only be given, not demanded. So asserting your own desires is the opposite of loving behavior. As well as longing to be true to yourself, you long to love and be loved, which means that you must find a way that combines being true to yourself with love.

As with people, so with possessions: by asserting your desires you seize what others do not possess, and so cut yourself off from them. You make yourself rich at the expense of other people, and you define happiness by the possession of goods that others do not have. Now these possessions can just as easily be spiritual goods as material goods. Jesus' parable of the Pharisee and the tax collector illustrates this point. "I thank you, Father, that I am not like this tax collector," says the Pharisee; "I'm not like him because I pray and fast and keep the commandments." Whereas the tax collector simply beats his breast and says: "Lord have mercy on me, a sinner." Which of the two is being more true to himself? We instinctively know that it is the tax collector. The pharisee defines himself as not like other people: this is the classic false self masquerading as the true self.

The parable is a good yardstick for measuring how true you are to yourself. When you can, without affectation, say: "I am a sinner," then the process of being true to yourself is really under way, because in saying so you recognize that the human heart is a place of evil desires as well as a place of good desires. A sense of personal sinfulness is a healthy reality check, to stop the false self getting away with being the true self. A sense of sin means that you do not trust yourself always to do the loving thing; you need some outside check on wayward desires. If you can accept that as a fact of life, then you can receive help and guidance and choose to obey it. In this way you can limit the sense of your own infallibility while still taking small steps along the road of self-realization. You will advance slowly and cautiously but with much less likelihood of being self-indulgent and with much less chance of damaging other people as you go.

This means, of course, that you have a greater chance of loving other people rather than simply using them as part of your self-expression. Your sense of sinfulness leads you beyond independence to reach out to other people for support. Beyond independence lies interdependence; you may freely choose to attach yourself to the life of another in a relationship or to others in a community. So the challenge is to be true to yourself in a loving way, and I believe that challenge is met most realistically by recognizing that you need forgiveness, guidance, and help to achieve it. Forgiveness, guidance, and help—all three find their richest source in God, so let's now turn again to look at prayer in this context. As Merton urges in the memorable title of one of his chapters: "Pray for your own discovery."

# PRAY FOR YOUR OWN DISCOVERY

In some modern psycho-spiritual writing there has been a tendency to equate inner desires with the voice of God; at the extreme, God becomes just a word that describes the collective interior world of humanity. But you cannot simply declare the inner world to be the same as God without emptying the word "God" of its classic meaning. Your interior life is one of the places where God will manifest his presence but the presence of God in the soul is not the same as divinizing desires. People cannot simply assert their true self; they need to pray for the strength to find that self beyond their desires.

In the earlier chapter on meditation, the prayer of the tax collector featured in a modified form as the Jesus Prayer, one of the phrases that can be repeated in meditation: "Lord Jesus Christ, have mercy on me, a sinner." It is significant that this is the most widely known Christian prayer mantra. It is a prayer that simultaneously highlights both the forgiveness of God and the self-awareness of the one praying. In a very real sense, to pray that prayer is to engage in prayer as "being true to myself." The sinner knows two things for sure: I am a sinner, and God forgives me. Taken together, those are two very precious certainties; here I have found out how to be true to myself in a loving way, only the loving way starts with God's love for me, not my love for others.

88

Let's now look again at the powerful question about who sets the agenda in your life. As you "pray for your own discovery," the agenda of your life is set neither by other people nor by yourself; it is set by God. Life becomes the search for God's agenda in your life. When you find it, then you have found your true self. You have found the ultimate obedient freedom. To find this agenda is the work of a lifetime and it cannot be done alone. To do it you must stay in the sanctuary and not give up when the bad weather comes, as it inevitably will. The walls of obedience need a roof to hold them together, and to offer shelter against the elements. You cannot build this roof on your own: you need to accept other people's help. This requires humility, which is the next step. The paradox is that you climb up to the roof by the way of humility.

## Further steps toward obedience

*On the web:* www.mertonfoundation.org is a web site that offers a wide range of resources to help you find out about Thomas Merton's life and writings.

*In a book: Seeking God: The Way of Benedict* is a good introduction to applying the Benedictine way to ordinary life written by Esther de Waal, an Anglican laywoman.

# STEP 4:
# Humility

*We descend by exaltation and we ascend
by humility.*

Rule of St. Benedict, 7: "Humility"

"Eating humble pie" sounds like an unpleasant experience, yet the monastic tradition insists that humility is a quality that enriches our lives. So we need to begin by asking ourselves what we do and do not mean by "humble." It is probably easier to begin by saying what humility does *not* mean, so let's start by considering an infamously humble individual, Uriah Heep. This famous Dickensian character appears in the novel *David Copperfield* and the phrase "I'm ever so 'umble" is constantly on his lips. He is an odious character, who pretends to be subservient toward his elders while constantly plotting the downfall of his employer. He is eventually unmasked by Mr. Micawber and he gets his comeuppance, but his portrayal is so vivid and his catchphrase so memorable that it has left being "ever so 'umble" with a rather tarnished reputation. Uriah Heep has come to symbolize humility as insincere groveling. While Uriah may be a caricature, there are more subtle misrepresentations of humility that also need to be set aside if we are to discover its true meaning.

First, being humble is often seen as being passive—just accepting things and not complaining when something bad happens. But this is apathy and inaction rather than humility. Second, humility can be understood as a character trait, possessed by some but unnatural for others. This view associates humility with people who are quiet or introverted by temperament. Seen in this way, humility is not for everyone. Finally, being humble is seen as characteristic of the elderly, especially women. This is summed up in the use of the phrase "a little old lady," which immediately conjures up a picture of mild mannered, mousy behavior. Putting these together, we get a definition of humility as passive behavior by timid people. Yet such a definition is superficial and misleading, as a simple story illustrates. Nursing staff in a hospital were concerned by an elderly patient who said little and seemed very passive; seeing the chaplain pass by, a nurse asked him to go and have a word with the man. When the chaplain spoke to him, the old man replied vigorously: "Bugger off, vicar; I'm not dead yet." Was this man quiet, angry and humble? Or was he quiet, angry and aggressive? Or neither? The fact is that simply observing passive, quiet behavior indicates neither the presence nor the absence of humility.

Looking beyond the purely personal, some societies can appear to be built on humility. Some cultures involve the enforced submission of younger to elder, of women to men, of one race to another. But this submission should not be confused with humility. In such cultures people are not humbled, they are humiliated, and there is a world of difference between humility and humiliation. Humiliation is a misery, either self-inflicted or imposed; it includes a sense of shame on the part of the one humiliated; it is destructive. As the defense of human rights has become one of the defining values of a developed culture, so socially entrenched humiliation has become less and less acceptable around the world. The ending of apartheid in South Africa, the growth of feminism, legislation to protect the young and vulnerable—these twentieth-century movements have reduced the systematic humiliation that once dominated the lives of many people. Global awareness of the need to eliminate humiliation has contributed to people's fear that humiliation is what will happen to them if they pursue humility.

Humility is neither a specific behavior found in some people nor a behavior imposed by certain societies. Humility is a quality of life and a state of mind that has to be consciously developed. It has to be looked for as a gift from God and the ultimate act of humility is to ask God with all your heart for the gift of humility.

 EARTHLY ROOTS

As before, let's begin by examining the origin of the word in order to understand its true meaning. The root is the Latin word *humus,* which means "soil" or "earth." From this follows a very practical definition: to be humble is to be down-to-earth. This leads into being realistic, honest, and truthful. The root also connects humility to humanity, because to be human is to be made from the *humus. Homo sapiens* is the piece of earth that knows it is alive, an insight beautifully expressed in the book of Genesis. Adam is the name of the one made out of *admah,* the Hebrew word for the ground. He is *sapiens* because he has knowledge, is able to name things, and to choose which fruits of paradise to enjoy. But the one fruit he must not enjoy is the fruit of the tree of knowledge of good and evil. This knowledge would mean he was divine, because only God can judge good and evil. Yet the desire to be divine gets the better of both Adam and Eve; the serpent persuades them that God has told them a lie: "God has said that you will die if you eat the forbidden fruit, but," says the serpent, "you won't die, you'll be like gods." The temptation for Adam and Eve is to give up being of the *humus*—humble and human—and to become gods, the ultimate act of pride. This lack of humility and humanity is their downfall: paradise is lost.

This story is played out in the life of each human being, as people struggle to be down-to-earth and avoid the temptation to act as if they were the divine center of the universe. If you examine human interactions that go wrong, whether in bitter arguments or wars, there is usually somewhere a lack of humility and an excess of arrogance. So this chapter on humility is about our struggle to be fully human, about the desire to be rooted in the real earthly self and not to be deceived by the lie of the divine self. This basic human task is shared by people of all eras and all places, so when I'm asked if I believe in the Genesis creation story, I always reply that it is the truest story that I know.

# HUMILITY AND THE WILL TO SUCCEED

One of the world's best-selling business books is *From Good to Great* by the American Jim Collins. In this book, he answers one simple question: can a good company become a great company and, if so, how? Most great companies have a founding genius such as Walt Disney or Henry Ford. But what about the vast majority of companies that come to realize that they are good but not great? How can they become great? Collins and a team of over twenty researchers spent five years analyzing nearly fifteen hundred major companies to find the answer. They discovered that if I were to invest $1 in a range of Dow Jones Index companies, I would get back $56 after fifteen years. But if I invested that same dollar in a portfolio of companies that had moved from good to great, over the same period I would earn $470. So what are the common growth factors that the researchers discovered among the good-to-great companies?

The factors that they discovered were not what they expected. Take Kimberley-Clark, for example, which in 1971 was an old-fashioned paper company whose stock value had fallen drastically in the previous twenty years. In that year, a new CEO called Smith took over, a mild mannered in-house lawyer. Over the next twenty years he transformed the company into the world's leading manufacturer of paper-based consumer products with brands such as Kleenex, and it outperformed the stock market four times over. Smith was interviewed by a journalist who asked him to describe his management style. After an embarrassed silence he simply replied: "Eccentric." He was a shy man from a poor background, who played down his CEO status. Yet he had fierce resolve and a tremendous vision for the company.

What the researchers found was that the critical turning point in the fortunes of a good-to-great company coincided with the arrival of a CEO who blended "extreme personal humility with intense professional will." This was contrary to all common perceptions of a great CEO, who is pictured as thrusting and overbearing, ruthless and insensitive. The larger-than-life savior with the big personality is not the way to sustained greatness: humility is.

Alongside this humility there must be a strong will and ambition—ambition not for oneself but for the company. At the heart of humility there is real strength, and to be humble requires great inner resources. Somebody with humility must have learned how to handle their own emotions and how to touch the goodwill of other people in order to involve others in the project of building greatness. Then the will to greatness captures the energies of other people, rather than antagonizing them.

It was once my privilege to visit a man who had built up a business in just this way: his office was modest in size, with a round table in the middle surrounded by chairs and with nothing at all on the table. On a sideboard there was a phone, with some books, photos, and examples of his products. On the wall, some original works of art. This was the modest heart of a very powerful business. Here the owner said he could think, listen to his managers, and meet other people; the room spoke of space, calm, and focus. This was the humble will to succeed made manifest very concretely. And it reminded me of nothing so much as a sanctuary.

So at the heart of a truly great business there is a lack of busyness and the presence of a humble, determined visionary. The business world is often taken to be the place above all others where humility is seen as a liability rather than an asset. Yet the research by Collins and his team shows that this is not the case. They show that humility is a necessary quality in a CEO for a business to excel. So having established humility's credentials in the modern world, we are ready to see what the monastic tradition can tell us about how to live out this essential human quality.

## THE LADDER OF HUMILITY

As always, the desert fathers and mothers have some stories on the subject. A desert mother, Theodora, tells the story of a hermit who was able to banish demons. She asked the demons: "What drives you away from this holy hermit? Is it his fasting?" "We do not eat or drink," replied the demons. "So is it his vigils?" "We do not sleep," they replied. "Is it his separation from the world?" "Of course not; we live in deserts ourselves," said the demons. "So," asked Theodora, "what power drives you away then?" And the demons replied: "Nothing can overcome us, except humility."

As with Jim Collins, so with the desert tradition fifteen hundred years ago; we see how humility is uniquely strong and can drive out the demons that beset the human heart and lead it on to greatness.

In his Rule Benedict places humility at the heart of his insights about the monastic life. After his opening chapters on the different kinds of monks and on how to elect an abbot, Benedict turns to the heart of his teaching with a presentation of the three key qualities of the monastic life: obedience, silence, and humility. We have already looked at the first two and now we come to the last of the three. Benedict uses the image of a ladder to describe the way humility works in life. On this ladder, "we descend by exaltation and we ascend by humility." The ladder is our life, which will be raised to heaven if we have a humble heart. One side of the ladder is our body, the other is our soul, and the rungs are the steps of humility by which we ascend the ladder. There are twelve steps and at the top is found "perfect love," a place where there is delight in virtue and no fear. This summit of the ladder is deeply attractive but Benedict's twelve steps on how to get there make tough reading for modern minds. They are the product not only of Benedict's spiritual genius but also of Benedict's culture; so be warned: they can sometimes be distasteful to modern ears. Yet the five men in *The Monastery* learned to climb this ladder, and their climb will illustrate how much people today can learn from this demanding teaching.

The First Step of Humility is "fear of God," not in the sense of terror but in the sense of awe. Without a feeling for the awesome wonder of life we cannot begin our climb. Alongside experiencing awe, Benedict asks that the monk "flees all forgetfulness"; we must remember what life is all about and not try to escape from it. This mindful awe will lead us to take life seriously, to see life as a task to be lived with a sense of deep purpose. Paradoxically, a sense of humor is essential if life is to be taken seriously, but the humor must be directed at our own folly and not at life itself. To put it another way, if life is deeply serious, then much of our superficial living is a joke. Some contemporary attitudes seem to imply the reverse: the serious pursuit of personal pleasure at all costs is often combined with a frivolous attitude to life itself. This is the mindless hedonism of "sex, drugs, and rock 'n' roll": life is a joke and we're seriously intent on blotting out life's absurdity. By contrast, if we can see how serious life is and laugh at our own foolishness, then we will have made a start on the first rung of the ladder of humility. For the five television men, simply coming on the forty-day retreat meant that they had already taken this first step, and it was that serious intention combined with a sense of humor that enabled them to make so much spiritual progress.

The Second Step of Humility "is that a monk does not love his own will or delight in the satisfaction of his own desires." The dominance of self-expression in our contemporary culture makes this sound strange. To do your own thing and to express yourself are accepted as self-evidently good, and much modern spirituality is seen as an extension of this. Yet the human heart is a place of many desires, some of them contradictory. This Second Step of Humility invites us to recognize that, insofar as our lives are dedicated to pleasing ourselves, then they are doomed to frustration. People who contrive constantly to get their own way are neither popular nor happy. The real delight in life comes from the acceptance of realities other than one's own—the reality of the other person's needs and the reality that some things should be accepted as they are.

The acceptance of these realities brings real peace, but such an attitude of acceptance is not easy to acquire: I must learn to put a break between my own desires and my actions, between the thought and the deed, in order to allow other factors to enter the equation. For example, if I'm hungry, I eat. But if I learn to wait before eating, in the discipline called fasting, then the link between desire and action is slowed. This traditional religious discipline has much to commend it, but here I offer it as an example of how we can learn to become more reflective in our response to desire. By waiting before sating my craving for food I learn to contain my desires. Obviously our desires never disappear, nor should we want them to; that is the error of puritan religion.

What we can do, however, is learn to allow factors other than personal cravings to dictate our actions. Gluttony and greed, lust and vanity, avarice and anger—these and the other desires of the heart are permanent features of life, but they can be contained so that we react more slowly to them and allow other factors a role in our choices.

In the Third Step of Humility Benedict opens up the soul to those other factors that we can obey when we have learned to slow down our reactions to our cravings. In this step, "A monk for the love of God submits to his superior in all obedience." As we saw in the last chapter, this is not the military obedience required for the good functioning of an army, but rather the obedience required for a family or community to be a place of love. This is a concrete way of setting aside our desires and is an expression of freedom.

The Fourth Step of Humility reveals how the previous step benefits not just the family or community but also the one who is obedient: "In this obedience under difficult, unfavorable, or even unjust conditions, his heart quietly embraces suffering"; this last word being *patientiam* in the original, so I would say "embraces patience." Humility involves patience and that is why it provides a good opportunity for personal growth. Patience is not the same as tolerance, since some things should not be tolerated. But all things should be dealt with patiently; an overhasty response is rarely helpful, even in a crisis. But nor is patience simply grinning and bearing things we hate; that is endurance. Patience is more subtle: it is the attempt to live out in a positive frame of mind the difficulties that come from trying to obey and love other people. To embrace patience is indeed to embrace suffering, but a suffering undertaken out of love. The conflicts and arguments experienced by the men in *The Monastery* were indications of people struggling to take this step. The fact that Anthoney nearly left after an argument but actually pulled back at the last minute was a huge step on to the fourth rung of the Ladder of Humility. He chose patient obedience to the group over his craving to "get out of here."

The Fifth Step of Humility "is that a man does not conceal from his abbot any evil thoughts entering his heart, or any wrongs committed in secret, but rather confesses them humbly." This has been called "radical self-honesty" and it is a key feature of the monastic tradition. In *The Monastery* the five men began to live out this step in their dialogues with their monastic teachers and mentors. Their openness enabled them to grow and to learn at a remarkable rate; these dialogues were deeply affecting in their honesty and the way they helped the men to move forward.

The dialogues could be regarded as a kind of psychotherapy and there are indeed overlapping features. But notice that here the emphasis is not on one's psyche but on sinful thoughts and wrongful actions. While counseling is nonjudgmental and therapy attempts to engage with personal history, this humble confession of faults is a personal critique of current behavior. Just as there is a place for counseling and therapy, so there is a place for confession.

Now this can be read as fostering guilt and being negative, but the paradox is that being honest about the negative parts of one's life can be a very positive experience. It is positive because it lets light into dark places. My experience as a priest is that, far from making somebody feel guilty, admitting to a wrong they have done releases people from their guilt and enables them to move forward. The desert fathers saw the failure to speak out one's sins to another as the devil's best way of keeping somebody in the grip of evil. "Nothing so heartens the devil as when his imaginations are kept secret," says the desert tradition.

Such openness needs to be met by good listening and wise direction, which is why Benedict commends the abbot as the right person, since Benedict presumes such qualities in the abbot. Obviously others might be equally effective, although care needs to be taken over whom to trust. This monastic tradition of the open acknowledgement of evil thoughts and deeds is one of the roots of the Catholic tradition of sacramental confession to a priest.

The next three steps make more sense when they are seen in the light of the radical self-honesty of the previous step. The Sixth, Seventh, and Eighth Steps are all about self-abasement and self-abasement needs to be seen as part of self-honesty. Seen as self-inflicted humiliation, self-abasement is pointless and even dangerous. But seen as a continuation of personal honesty, it is of great value. The Sixth Step "is that the monk is content with the lowest and most menial treatment and regards himself as a poor and worthless workman in whatever task he is given." Like "poor," "worthless" is a relative term meaning "less worthy" rather than "of no worth." The emphasis here, however, should be on contentment: the ability to be content whatever happens to you is the fruit of great self-awareness. Even when status is taken away, the humble person can live fruitfully and happily.

The Seventh Step "is that a man not only admits with his tongue but is also convinced in his heart that he is inferior to all and of less value." What is significant here is the emphasis on inner conviction. I once came across a wonderful Victorian guide to good manners containing a section that mirrored this step. The section was entitled "Vicious Humility" and described how some people begin a conversation by saying something like: "Well of course I am no expert but it seems to me . . ." or "Ignorant as I am, I hesitate to express an opinion . . ." These opening phrases are "vicious" because they are false humility; as Benedict puts it, the speaker "only admits with the tongue." If the speaker really believed his opening gambit, he would keep silent. What the speaker is doing, paradoxically, is gaining your approval for his opinion; by pretending it is worthless, he hopes you will affirm that the opinion is in fact correct with a "Come, come, sir, you do yourself an injustice; that is a sound opinion." Such "vicious" humility is the target of this step.

The Eighth Step "is that a monk does only what is endorsed by the common rule of the monastery and the example set by his superiors." This sounds awful to modern ears, a recipe for stagnation and oppression, something that no creative young person should contemplate as part of their life. A Vietnamese Buddhist abbot once confronted this culture clash head-on when visiting a U.S. university in the 1960s. He was asked how he instructed foreign students who visited him to learn the way of enlightenment. He replied simply: "I tell them to make the tea." Somehow we have to arrive at a point where we recognize that spiritual learning is going to enter deeply into our souls and that we will kick against this learning. The Adam and Eve in each of us will want to be in charge and will want too much knowledge of good and evil. We would prefer to learn on our own terms, in our own way, but the spiritual life is not like that: make the tea, say the prayers, and listen to the elders, not simply as a way to put you down but to help you grow away from self-will toward a new framework of life where God can speak. Another way to illuminate this step is to view it from the side of the superiors. This places a huge responsibility on them to make the right demands for the community and to live it out fully. In a good community they will ask all members to contribute to working out how to apply the common rule.

The Ninth, Tenth, and Eleventh Steps all deal with the restraint of speech and, while we have already seen what the monastic tradition has to say about silence, here in these steps Benedict shows how silence flows from community life as outlined in the Eighth Step. In family and community life people can waste a huge amount of time and energy complaining about the management, grumbling about the conditions, and gossiping maliciously. Benedict hates grumbling and forbids it above all other vices: "Above all, let them not grumble," he says. He also dislikes certain kinds of laughter; he knows that people can get into a pattern of jokey behavior that is not the self-deprecating humor that helps life move forward gently but the crude laughter that leads to malicious behavior and bullying. None of this has any place in a good family, a good community, or a good workplace.

With all these steps below us, we now stand on the top rung of the ladder. The Twelfth Step is for a monk's humility to be evident "in his bearing no less than in his heart." This can be summarized as integrity, so that the outer and the inner person are at one, with no dissimulation of mind or body. The humble person is known by the combination of both physical and personal attitude. And what is this attitude? Nothing spectacular and nothing heroic, simply the realization: "Lord, I am a sinner"; and so Benedict concludes with a reference to the parable of the tax collector and the pharisee. At the top of Benedict's ladder is a person who has literally ascended by falling: the constant mindfulness of sin is the top rung. On this final step the monk's mindfulness of his faults is a source of joy because it reminds him of God's mercy and how much God loves him. He will have faults like all people, but his distinguishing mark is a deep awareness of his own faults, a lack of complaint about the faults of others, and a constant singing of God's praises in thankfulness for mercy. Having climbed the ladder, he has come back down to earth, ascending by falling.

In many ways, "ascending by falling" describes the experience Tony had at the end of *The Monastery*—not so much a religious experience of exaltation as a religious experience of coming down to earth. During the previous weeks, he had allowed himself to climb many of the steps on the Ladder of Humility and this work had brought him closer to his own humanity, away from some of the humanly degrading things he had been doing before. At the end of his stay, in his final session with his mentor, he wondered what he was going to do when he returned home. Then, in a moment of grace, he stepped onto the top rung and that brought him back to earth, with a great sense of joy at being there. And there he has remained since the program, happily grounded, more grounded as each week goes by and delighted to have rediscovered his humanity through the mercy of God. With real integrity, he has put one way of life behind him and moved onto another, combining personal humility with a strong will to succeed.

# *Further steps toward humility*

*On the web:* Go to www.worthabbey.net/bbc and click on "Tony's Story" for his own compelling account of what happened to him during his forty days in the monastery.

*In a book: Truthful Living* by Michael Casey, an Australian Trappist monk, who examines St. Benedict's teaching on humility in depth. The inspiration for much of this chapter.

# STEP 5:

# Community

*They should each try to be the first to show respect to each other, supporting with the greatest patience one another's weaknesses of body or behavior.*

Rule of St. Benedict, 72: "The Good Zeal of Monks"

Let's take stock of how far we have come in finding sanctuary. I have suggested that we enter the sanctuary through the door marked "Virtue," that we then have to work at laying down a floor of silence and meditation, upon which we can build up the ability to listen to God. We ended Step 3 on "Obedience" by asking how to find shelter from the elements. In answer to that question, we have climbed the Ladder of Humility and have reached the roof. This is a place of shelter, where Benedict says fear is cast out and perfect love is possible. So let's see how he makes good this possibility of love by looking at what he says about community.

## ⬥— COMMUNITY AND ME —⬥

A concept is in trouble when it is used freely by politicians, and community is just such a concept. The ease with which something is declared to be a community is now quite extraordinary. For example, here are some communities mentioned recently by politicians in newspaper articles: people who ride bicycles are "the cycling community," spies and their masters are "the intelligence community," and people with the same ethnic origin are "the black community." Nobody denies that all these groups of people have something distinctive in common: bikes, spying, and race. But in what sense do such common factors actually make a diverse group of people into a community? For me the low point of this ever-expanding notion of community came when an IT consultant asked me to explain how we managed "our database community." When I asked him what that was, he said it was all the people whose details we had on our database; apparently, simply having their names and addresses on the same computer disk now turns people into a community.

Thus, although a neighborhood is often referred to as "the local community," all too often this only means a shared zip code rather than a shared life. The problem lies in the fact that "community" has at least two different meanings and people like to cash in on the good feeling generated by one meaning when in fact they mean the other. So, for example, when somebody buys a bike, they are joining a community in the following sense: a group of people with a common identifying feature. But when somebody joins a cycling club they are joining a community in a different sense: a group of people who have the specific intention of engaging with others who have a similar interest. Very often people want to claim that their community is the latter when in fact it is only the former. So by buying a bike I can claim to have joined a community without having to do the more demanding work of engaging personally with other people: I literally buy community on the cheap.

The reason for this is that people tend to see themselves first and foremost as independent individuals who only become related to others in limited ways. So today's autonomous individuals choose cautiously to join a few organizations with limited aims, such as a sports club. Beyond that, most people choose only a small circle of family, friends, and colleagues with whom they really engage; fewer and fewer people are engaging with large communities. The comradeship of the political party and the trade union has given way to the mutually convenient political or social alliance. The fellowship of the church has been overtaken by the individual desire for spiritual comfort. The literal love of neighbor has been replaced by local conciliation services to resolve neighborhood disputes. While some new communities sprang up in the sixties and seventies, many communities of mutual support are ebbing away. In Britain today most people under the age of thirty do not join political parties, do not go to church, and do not give to charity. Many young people do not even bother to vote.

In 2005 MTV produced a marketing report entitled: "Is this the most 'Me' generation ever?" The report showed that the growing sophistication of electronic gadgetry has led to a generation connected to their machines rather than to each other; the global village is fading as people have more potential to be better informed but couldn't care less. The hyper-consumer is young and confident, and acquires self-esteem by buying well, rather than by the boring process of acquiring wisdom. People are increasingly connected to their own story, not to anybody else's.

Even allowing for exaggeration, this report made me realize that we are in danger of creating a world in which "I am my own sanctuary." So let's consider what Benedict offers to help people escape from the dead end of "self-sanctuary" and engage more widely in the task of building real communities.

## ✦——— BENEDICTINE COMMUNITY ———✦

This tendency to "self-sanctuary" is found among the more spiritually minded as well as among the electronically connected. During one of the dialogues the Worth community have had recently with the Buddhist monks of Chithurst, we were discussing community life. The Buddhist abbot told us that considerable numbers of people who came to him said they wanted to live as hermits; they did not want to live with the other monks but wanted to live on their own immediately. He pointed out to them that the Buddha has much to say about community life and about learning to live with others. Benedict's own life seems to have involved a similar excess of zeal for the hermit life: he left Rome as a student and went into the hills east of Rome to seek God on his own, in a cave. While the Rule allows for monks who want to live as hermits, this is only for those "who have come through the test of living in a monastery for a long time, and have passed beyond the first fervor of monastic life" (RB, 1:3). Benedict seems to have learned from his own youthful errors. In the struggle for purity of heart, the great monastic goal, our reactions to other people teach us a great deal about ourselves. Only when we have learned those lessons are we "ready with God's help to grapple single-handed with the vices of body and mind."

When a Benedictine monk or nun makes vows, they do not promise what many people think of as the traditional vows of poverty, chastity, and obedience. Those are the vows of orders such as the Franciscans, who sprang up in the Middle Ages, some seven hundred years after Benedict. The vows that Benedict invites his monks to take are those of Obedience, Stability, and one that is impossible to translate from Latin, *Conversatio morum*. It is easy to think that this last one reads *conversio,* in which case it would mean "conversion"; but scholars now agree that is not what Benedict intended. If you look up the word "conversation" in some dictionaries, you find a clue to the meaning of *conversatio*. There you discover that the first and now obsolete meaning of "conversation" is "living with somebody," and that the second but now normal meaning derives from this—namely "speaking with somebody." So this Benedictine vow is a resolution to live with others, specifically with other monks and hence to live the monastic way of life, with the implication of common ownership and celibacy. It is striking that all three Benedictine vows relate to community life: Benedictines promise to obey, to be stable, and to live with others in the monastic way. Some historians suggest that in fact Benedict saw these as just one vow: the promise to live one's whole life in obedience to this monastic community. Whether this is the case or not, there are clearly three dimensions to the vow and having looked at the meaning of obedience in the Third Step, let's now look more closely at the other two dimensions or vows.

The Benedictine vow of stability helps the monk avoid the temptation to believe that the grass is always greener on the other side of the fence. When discussing the different kinds of monks, Benedict is particularly critical of those known as "gyrovagues," "who spend their entire lives drifting from region to region, staying as guests for three or four days in different monasteries." He considers them to be "slaves to their own wills and gross appetites" (RB, 1:11). Benedict is clear that you can only grow in the spiritual life by staying not so much in one place but with one stable community. The experience of interacting with other people is central to his vision of spirituality, and there is evidence throughout the Rule that he knew this was the hardest part of that vision. His first edition of the Rule was probably shorter than the edition we now have, and the chapters he added later all deal with community relationships; there is nothing about the difficulties of prayer or the need to work harder, nothing about the administration of the monastery and its goods. Those were not the important practical difficulties that he faced when monks tried to live out his Rule; the major problems are presumably those dealt with in greater detail in the extra chapters added to the second edition of the Rule. This final section is all about community life: how to respond when asked to do the impossible, about not coming to blows, about obeying each other and not just the abbot, culminating in a one-sentence summary: "To their fellow monks they show the pure love of brothers; to God, loving fear; to their abbot, unfeigned and humble love. Let them prefer nothing whatever to Christ and may he bring us all together to everlasting life" (RB, 72:8–12). We get to heaven together or not at all; there are no private compartments on the Benedictine journey to everlasting life.

So for Benedict simply staying the course with other people is a vital step in spiritual living and hence the vow of stability, the vow to join a specific community for life. The other Benedictine vow relates to this very directly. As we've already noted, *conversatio morum* means living together and the English word "conversation" derives from that. If the stability of staying together is a key step, then actually talking to the people with whom you live is a vital part of that. Conversation is necessary for community to be real. Even though Benedict commends silence as a background, serious and deep conversation is also an essential part of spiritual living. As we saw in the chapter on humility, Benedict is rather puritan in his attitude to frivolous conversation, but in that same chapter he is equally clear about the need for good conversation.

## GOOD CONVERSATION
## IN PRACTICE

Whether helping people to deal with marital breakdown or with conflicts at work, I find that the need for good conversation is as relevant as ever in sustaining people in their communities. The busyness of their lives can lead people to neglect speaking directly to spouses or colleagues about serious matters; the superficial is always easier to talk about. People find it particularly hard to express their feelings about what is happening, and it is important to create a safe space within which people can express themselves. When I was working as the headmaster of our school, our management-team meetings ended with five minutes during which each person was asked to say what they had been feeling during the meeting. There was no discussion, just a series of statements by the participants; the convention was that you had to express your feelings about the meeting there and then, not behind people's backs. "I was annoyed when you cut across me" . . . "I really appreciated the way the group helped me to clarify that proposal" . . . "I was depressed by that financial report." These are examples of what people said, and it helped to ensure a deep sense of working together as complete human beings, saying the hard things if necessary and then moving on.

Good conversation requires not only good speaking but good listening. So in fact "restraint of speech" (the title of

Benedict's chapter on silence) is the essential corollary of good speaking, not its opposite. This is real community living and it is essential if human beings are to be their best selves. A community that generates a set of conventions for good conversation sets people free to give of their individual best.

One of the projects that we run within "The Open Cloister," Worth's retreat program, is "The Soul Gym." This project has involved writing about "Integrity in Practice" for the Financial Services Authority and running "Ethos Seminars" for managers. One such seminar involved a company's European management team, whose members were clearly searching for better ways to work together. We offered them a simple strategy during the seminar: make a request of your colleagues and make an offer to your colleagues. We invited them to take time to reflect and write down the main behaviors that they would like people to do (or avoid) and the ones that they would promote themselves. So, typically, a manager might say: "Please can regional managers share ideas more so that we can learn from each other; and I offer to be less defensive in the way I approach HQ." This simple device produced a new, deeper level of conversation in the seminar and most importantly a better set of working relationships afterward. This example illustrates how good conversation is often elusive but that the way to achieve it is often very simple; people just need active encouragement to express their individuality.

Benedict wants a community where people can express individuality rather than individualism. Individualism is simply doing your own thing in your own way and blanking out the other people. Individuality involves bringing your particular contribution to bear on the life of the community, even if that is a difficult contribution for others to accept; for example, a criticism. This "good speaking," as we might call it, is encouraged in Benedict's chapter "On Summoning the Brothers For Counsel," in which he also says, "The reason why we have said all should be called for counsel is that the Lord often reveals what is better to the younger." Everybody, even the youngest, must be encouraged to contribute.

In today's society there are encouraging signs of some people making a conscious effort to generate this kind of community life in new ways. Reading groups have recently experienced a resurgence of popularity, creating small communities where people can share good conversation. Amateur sports clubs are increasingly seen as being about more than sport; so, for example, the Worcester Joggers make the proud boast "We don't leave anybody behind," and they double back to pick up the tailenders. Peter Gilbert, a former director of social services, is a member and has written about his experience of the club in a mental-health journal. He believes that running puts people at the same level, so that the club becomes an extended family, sharing experiences and ideas, achievements and disappointments. Once again, good conversation happens when people decide to put in place proactive but simple means to generate it.

Such proactive and simple structures are what Benedict describes in much of his Rule. He creates a particular way of doing things in his community; he is happy for other abbots to modify these arrangements as they see fit, but there must be an *agreed* way of doing things. Without such an agreed way, real conversations are not possible; community life sustains good conversation by encouraging it and contains good conversation by setting boundaries. People know what to expect and what is expected of them. So the vows of stability and *conversatio* set up the expectation that people will persevere in community life and that they will sustain a high level of good conversation. Let's now look at the way a "rule" works to support these expectations.

## A RULE OF LIFE

For Benedict, monastic life means living under a rule and an abbot, where "rule" means a description of a whole way of life, not simply a single instruction or rule in the modern sense. To understand the role of a rule in community life, we must look at Pachomius, the first of the desert fathers to create a community. Originally these monks were all hermits, offering support to each other at a distance and living in very loose communities; as often happened, one day some young men came out into the

Egyptian desert to ask Pachomius for instruction in the monastic way.

Pachomius invited them to live with him so that he could teach them by his example. So he duly did all the chores, prayed profoundly and served the needs of the new brothers. He thought to himself that the newcomers would eventually get the hang of things and participate more fully in all that he was doing. Imagine his disappointment when these men showed that they were only too happy to let him do all the hard work. They even started to abuse him and exploit his apparent timidity. He allowed this to go on for several years, hoping that his humility would inspire them to change their ways; but they only abused his kindness all the more and as the years wore on, they came to despise Pachomius. He finally realized that something had to change, so he gave them a clearly stated description of the way of life that he expected them to lead. He laid down clearly how a monk should live and in this way created the first monastic rule for a community. He called his community a *koinonia,* a Greek word that is used in the Bible to describe the early Christian community. This word is not easy to translate, but it has overtones of warm fellowship between those who belong to a large group. It is good conversation on a large scale and is sometimes translated as "communion" in English, as in the expressions "communion with other people" and "communion with nature." By the time of Pachomius's death, monastic life as "communion" had established itself throughout Egypt, sometimes in monasteries comprising many hundreds of monks. Through what he learned about it from other monastic teachers, this communal monastic life was to inspire the young Benedict. He saw the need for a clearly stated communal framework if monastic life was to be fruitful; hence his insistence that monks must live "under a rule and an abbot" (RB, 1:2).

Now this story of Pachomius may seem to be of little relevance today, but as with humility, so with community—a piece of modern research has brought unexpected confirmation of ancient monastic insights.

A modern British research team comprising a psychiatrist, a therapist, and a social worker noticed that much work had been done in researching one-to-one relationships and family relationships, but that very little research had been done on relationships within a large group. So in the 1980s they set up a large group (defined as more than twenty people) and simply watched it meet and develop over a number of years.

They observed that, after polite preliminaries, the first emotion to break out in the group was hate. Through family life, people had learned how to behave one-to-one and in a small group, but nobody had the skill of working in a large group. So the participants felt disempowered by the presence of large numbers of people, and they translated this frustration into hatred for particular people and for the group in general. At this stage the group began to talk about their hates, and out of this frank dialogue there emerged a set of conventions that all agreed to observe to enable the large group to work. After some years of working at it, they succeeded in creating their own culture and rules, within which the members felt able to work together harmoniously. They had created what I called earlier "conventions for good conversation."

Examination of their research in more detail shows that the first phase—hate—was full of self-absorbed and mindless behavior—people saying pretty awful things about each other. They were able to get out of this phase only when they looked beyond themselves and became more mindful; then they could consciously create the new culture that set them all free to develop their own communal ethos.

The researchers called this final stage *koinonia* and, though they knew this word was used in the Bible to describe the early church, they were unaware that it was the name also given to the first Christian monastic communities. Their group had moved from hate to dialogue to the creation of an explicit culture, following the same process as Pachomius had gone through in the creation of his first *koinonia*.

## COMMUNITY AS SANCTUARY

The five men discovered much of this during their time in the monastery, very particularly through the arguments that they had, some of which were very strong and one of which nearly led to blows. Some viewers told us they thought that these scenes were an unnecessary descent into the *Big Brother* television format, to which I replied that Benedict knew all about violent conflict in community long before television. Benedict actually has a chapter entitled "On the Presumption of Striking Another Monk" (RB, 70). It is there presumably because monks hitting each other was not unknown in a monastery, and so Benedict needed to point out that it was wrong.

The working through of such conflicts illustrates the difference between tranquillity and peace. In the chapter on prayer, we've already seen that serious prayer leads to an initial tranquillity but that this soon gives way to a struggle for peace. Both the ancient and the modern examples above show this in operation in human relationships. People have to build peace in relationships and they do so by creating relationships founded on fairness and respect. This fairness operates personally in our immediate family, in our local community, and globally. So, for example, there is no peace in a neighborhood if there is racial discrimination. Yet the greatest test of building peace is how we react to unfair treatment at the hands of others. We need to respond to such treatment not only fairly but also compassionately; only then do we really build peace. Hating our enemies, for example, does not build peace. We must resist injustice, but the high calling of peace-building invites us not to hate those who perpetrate it. This is extraordinarily demanding, but many twentieth-century religious figures offer fine examples. Mahatma Gandhi, Martin Luther King, and their movements of nonviolent resistance are the outstanding ones.

This demanding task of loving enemies requires a deep spiritual maturity, which involves a discipline of the spirit that is built up day by day. For Benedict, the greatest obstacles to true community living are murmuring and grumbling; he allows monks to point out what is wrong to the people responsible, as seen in the chapter of the Rule about how a brother should respond when asked to do the impossible. But complaining well is not the same as grumbling, which is a variant on hate and involves destructive words. "Above all else," says Benedict, "we admonish them to refrain from grumbling" (RB, 40:9). Grumbling is the opposite of good conversation; it is the denial of the vow of *conversatio morum* and so is prohibited in the strongest terms. The abbot is frequently admonished to ensure that nothing gives legitimate grounds for complaint because that becomes the seedbed of grumbling. If the legends about his life recorded by Gregory the Great are to be believed, Benedict knew about the destructive power of grumbling at first hand. The story goes that a group of monks invited him to be their abbot. They had heard of his great holiness and so they asked him to come and lead them, but they were very lax monks and he was much stricter than they had imagined, so they decided to get rid of him; they handed him a poisoned chalice from which to drink. As Benedict took the chalice, he blessed it and at that moment it shattered, spilling the poisoned wine on the ground. So Benedict was saved.

This legend has some striking elements: the ability of once well-intentioned monks to lose the plot so badly in community life that they plan a murder; the way that Benedict is saved from this evil not by cursing but by blessing. Within this story of evil grumbling and holy blessing is found the attitude that Benedict fosters in his community. Benedict knows that people will not always rise to the challenges of community life, so the abbot "must hate faults but love the brothers" (RB, 64:11). Obstacles are to be overcome by love as well as by discipline.

As the five men worked through their conflicts, they learned a great deal about how to make community work. Gary learned to be less aggressive, Anthoney to be less defensive; they all learned how to be peacemakers. Properly contained, conflict is a moment of learning for those involved; but there have to be safeguards in order to ensure everybody's well-being, which is where the chapter about not hitting people is important. The community both forms and protects its members—forming them in communal sensitivity and protecting them from other people's insensitivity. In response to this individual formation and protection, the members form and protect the community. This mutual activity of forming and protecting is the means by which a community becomes a sanctuary. Community is not just a flying buttress supporting the sanctuary; at its best, it is itself part of the sanctuary.

Community is in this way sacramental—that is to say, the material realities of community are the means by which the hidden grace of Christ is given to the members. God gives us the grace of obedience, restraint of speech, and humility through the community. These three qualities are not called virtues by Benedict, who would have understood virtues in the classical sense: fortitude and justice, temperance and prudence. Within the classical world of Benedict's time, virtues such as these were understood as habits that could be acquired through practice: a person could learn to be just and prudent through upbringing and education—habits that were kept for life. Obedience, silence, and humility, however, are qualities that we experience through faithfully persevering in community life; that is what a community is for: to foster the experience of these qualities through its very structures. For Benedict, once you are outside community, then these qualities are in danger of evaporating.

## RITUAL

One of the ways that Benedict puts in place these community structures is through ritual. Ritual and symbol get a bad press these days and are often accompanied by the word "mere," as in: "It's merely a symbol," or "mere ritual." Our society's qualms over ritual are a hindrance to community living. For example, nowadays, large numbers of teenagers never sit down to a family meal; that ritual has been lost and family life is weakened as a result. For Benedict, a shared meal, even in silence, is a vital part of community life, and in monasteries this basic ritual has other rituals added to it. The kitchen servers are given a blessing in front of the community and they are reminded that "such service increases reward and fosters love" (RB, 35:2). At the same time he tells them to eat before they serve so that "at the mealtime, they may serve their brothers without grumbling" (RB, 35:13). This combination of the symbolic and the practical is typical of Benedict and shows how the blending of ritual and mundane elements is both possible and desirable: the symbolic lifts the mundane to give it meaning without detracting from the need to do the mundane things well. To strengthen community life, you might consider developing rituals around the ordinary.

Returning to the joggers who have a custom of always going back for the tailenders: this is a ritual around the ordinary that speaks volumes about their vision of their club as an inclusive community. With imagination, we could all find ways of developing similar rituals in unexpected ways. Small rituals can transform ordinary events into powerful ways to build community.

In the Rule, this is seen most noticeably in the elaborate arrangements that Benedict proposes for receiving guests. When guests arrive ("and a monastery is never without them" [RB, 53:16]), the monks wash their feet, the abbot prays with them, and then reads the Bible to them; a special kitchen is set aside for guests and a monk is assigned to look after their accommodation. The need to avoid cause for grumbling because of all this extra work is specifically recognized and so extra help is made available if needed. This routine summarizes the community life of prayer and service, and it is all brought to bear on the guest, in whom "Christ is to be adored." Benedict emphasizes that all this applies especially to the poor: "Great care and concern are to be shown in receiving poor people and pilgrims, because in them more particularly Christ is received; our very awe of the rich guarantees them special respect" (RB, 53:15).

Yet at the end of the chapter on guests Benedict insists that these special arrangements should not disrupt the regular life of the community. He has carefully built up his monastery as a sanctuary of prayer and silence; he has arranged everything so that there is good order, so that the monks have nothing to grumble about. Nobody is admitted as a novice without some serious testing, but life is so arranged that a guest can be welcomed generously as a matter of course and without any disruption. In this way Benedict maintains a balance between the internal needs of the sanctuary and the external demands placed upon it. Ritual makes this possible for families as well so that, for example, a visitor can be welcomed to a family meal both easily and graciously, whereas simply feeding the guest is both disruptive and not very hospitable. A test of the sanctuary's strength is its ability to welcome guests without the whole structure being shaken—a fine balance.

This balancing act teaches us that real community is an inclusive rather than an exclusive step.

## ◆——  RICH AND POOR ALIKE  ——◆

Benedict insists that the members of his community not only love each other but that they must also go out of their way to love the visitor, especially the poor visitor, in whom Christ is adored. As we build sanctuary into our lives we must create space not only for our own needs but also for the needs of others, especially the needs of the poorest. That seems a tall order for people who are too busy doing too much and who may already find many of the suggestions I have made too demanding. But remember Benedict's brilliant balancing act; while we may not be able to copy it, we can find our own expression of it. The monastic tradition insists that as we make room for stillness and prayer, new possibilities in life are opened up and one of these is responding more generously to the needs of others. Somehow we have to enable the neediest to become members of our community with a valued place in our sanctuary.

This demand applies to those in need at home and abroad, but the challenge of those abroad is particularly daunting. The dilemma with which we began this book was that of the comparatively wealthy consumer in the developed world seeking refuge from his own consumerist culture. Yet alongside that there is an equally significant problem of the poor in the developing world also seeking refuge. They seek refuge not from consumerism but from poverty and they do so increasingly by emigrating to wealthy countries. I refer here not to those seeking political asylum but to those who migrate out of economic envy, those economic migrants who are attracted to our wealth. These economic migrants often claim to be seeking political asylum but that is irrelevant here. These are people seeking economic sanctuary within a global economic system that also leaves the poor in a state of being too busy. The experience of our monks working in one of the shanty towns of Lima, Peru has shown me at first hand that the poor are also too busy, though in the case of the poor they are too busy surviving rather than too busy consuming. The early start to cross the city in search of work, the chasing after a few pennies, the desperate search for medicines for sick children and, at the end of the day, fearful and fitful sleep—it is no wonder people seek refuge and try to escape from such situations.

The developed world responds by erecting bigger barriers to prevent the immigration of the envious poor, worried that they will upset the consumer/producer society's economic and social coherence. Until the world's economic system evolves to reduce poverty in the Third World, the migration of poor people is going to increase. How to provide enough sanctuary for rich and poor alike is a personal and social challenge on a global scale, one of the great challenges facing humanity in the twenty-first century.

The community we need to build as part of our sanctuary must embrace the poor outsider—such a vital principle for Benedict—both by working to create a global community where poverty is reduced and by welcoming him into our local community in some way.

## WINDOWS

Thus the kind of community we envisage is best described as the windows of the building: they protect us from the elements, yet they also allow us to see other people and let in the light of their presence. We can see their needs and communicate with them; we can also open the door of the sanctuary, the door of our hearts, and let them in. If our sanctuary has no windows, it will be a dark and gloomy place. So, like good builders, we need to balance out the need for windows with the need for strong walls. The strong walls of obedience need the windows of community to ensure that our sanctuary is bright and welcoming.

## *Further steps toward community*

*On the web:* www.laybenedictines.org is the web site of the Lay Community of St. Benedict, a group of laypeople who live out the Rule, based in Britain with members worldwide. www.thesoulgym.org offers insights about creating the right ethos at work.

*In a book: Prayer and Community* by Columba Stewart is a short book on Benedictine living, written by an American monk who has a profound grasp of the monastic tradition.

# STEP 6:
# Spirituality

*Test the spirits to see if they are from God.*

First letter of St. John, quoted in the Rule of St. Benedict, 58

The sanctuary is now nearly complete. As with all new buildings, however, we have to decide on the furniture and fittings. What other items should be in our sanctuary? What will fit and what will be out of place? A trip to the local household goods and furniture store is the usual material answer and there are plenty of spiritual equivalents around, in the form of Mind Body Spirit sections of bookshops and even Mind Body Spirit fairs.

Since the 1960s increasing numbers of people have turned to spirituality rather than religion as a source of solace and to find sanctuary from the busy consumer world. People are eager to express their spirituality and to promote spirituality in society. So as we decide what else might fit in our sanctuary, we need to look carefully at these spiritual offerings and choose wisely.

What people mean when they use the word "spirituality" varies enormously. When somebody says that they are spiritual this could mean that they enjoy meditation or that they like to go for solitary walks. Or it could mean that they appreciate great art or that they love music. Above all, it usually means that they believe in the infinite value of human love; for growing numbers of people to be making such an affirmation is impressive. They want to give expression to the invisible features of life that lie beyond the measurable world of science, believing that if they do, they will experience a greater sense of well-being.

These growing spiritual aspirations usually lack any clearly defined forms of expression, however, and many people are looking for guidance on how to be truly spiritual. They say that they know there is more to life than the busy round of consumption/production, but they do not know where to find this "more." The viewers' responses to *The Monastery* illustrated this, with literally thousands of people contacting us to say how helpful the program had been and asking for more guidance. For example: "I am an atheist doctor, but your TV program touched me deeply"; or "I feel lost and your program has given me a sense of purpose." Many went on to come to Worth on retreat, and our retreat center was quickly booked up months in advance.

In Europe, most people no longer look to the faithful practice of one religion to help them find "the spiritual more to life," and America may soon follow suit. So as we begin to consider the many spiritual movements on offer today, we need to understand how people have moved away from religion to spirituality. To do this, we need to trace the history of spirituality in western culture, going back to the time when religion and spirituality were indistinguishable.

## THE HISTORY OF SPIRITUALITY

To go back to Christian origins, St. Paul writes about the spiritual life as meaning "of the Spirit of God," and he contrasts the strength of spiritual living with the frailty of human nature. Christians are people who have the mind of Christ; they do spiritual things in accordance with Christ's spirit. This spirituality is seen in acts of love and generosity, whereas he describes the signs of unspiritual living as quarrels, greed, and selfishness. So for the early church, spiritual meant godly and generous living.

From the third century onward the meaning of spirituality took a new turn. Rather than seeing the spiritual as involving the whole of life, Christians now emphasized the distinction between body and soul. This was a view most commonly identified with the philosophy of Plato, which saw the soul as representing a higher level of life than the body. This body–soul distinction became deeply embedded in the European outlook and persists to this day in the phrase "a Platonic relationship." Spirituality became disconnected from the physical, and private; by the Middle Ages this distinction dominated not only private life but also public life. The body–soul split was institutionalized and every aspect of life was divided between the temporal and spiritual realms. This meant that part of government was in the hands of the Church (the Lords Spiritual) and part was in the hands of the State (the Lords Temporal).

The Protestant reformers of the sixteenth and seventeenth centuries believed that the church was exercising a power that was decidedly not spiritual; they considered it worldly and corrupt. To counteract this corruption they invited Christians to concentrate on the interior world of faith and not to rely on the external works of religion such as pilgrimages, shrines, and indulgences. In parallel to this Protestant reform there was a stirring of reform within the Catholic Church itself, with movements promoting the interior life of the soul. In sixteenth-century Spain Catholic pioneers such as Teresa of Avila and Ignatius Loyola generated a new wave of interior religious observance that is still felt to this day. Ignatius's legacy was not only the founding of the Society of Jesus (the Jesuits) but also his method of interior meditation called the *Spiritual Exercises*. Ignatius distilled his own religious experience into guidelines for spiritual growth, where "spiritual" takes on the sense of "interior and personal" rather than referring to the external observances of conventional religion. So, surprisingly, the founder of the Jesuits is one of the first people to use the word "spiritual" with its modern meaning.

Of course the leaders of the Reformation would have been horrified to think that their reform movement had started the process that led to the modern practice of being "spiritual but not religious." The Protestant and the Catholic reformers alike were promoting true religion—religion of the heart rather than the religion of convention and conformity that they saw around them. Their aim was to promote spiritual religion, and the separation of the two aspects was to them unthinkable. So how have we ended up separating the two?

It was at the start of the twentieth century that spirituality acquired its current meaning as something that could be separated from religion. While such a shift occurred gradually, there was nevertheless one crucial moment in this development. In 1902 the American psychologist and philosopher William James published *Varieties of Religious Experience,* in which he examined religion in a new way, from the psychological perspective and from inside the experience of the believer. He divided religion into two parts: "I propose to ignore the institutional branch entirely . . . Religion, therefore, as I now ask you arbitrarily to take it, shall mean for us the feelings, acts, and experiences of individual men in their solitude, so far as they apprehend themselves in relation to whatever they may consider the divine." This distinction captured the imagination of many people and became formalized into a widely accepted distinction in the modern understanding of religion. The experiences of individuals were one thing and institutionalized religion was another. These personal experiences were subjected to increasingly intense analysis by the newly developing science of psychology during the twentieth century and, by the end of the century, had become something quite separate from organized religion.

## SPIRITUAL BUT NOT RELIGIOUS

This movement to separate spirituality and religion has had a number of effects beyond simply creating the distinction. One of the most significant effects has been the emergence of a belief in western society that the institutional part of religion is optional—that real spirituality is a wholly private event and that this inward part is more or less the same across all religions and all people.

A typical modern explanation of this view is seen in the work of psychologist Abraham Maslow (famed for "Maslow's Triangle," his theory about the hierarchy of needs). In the 1970s Maslow conducted psychological research into "peak" experiences, which he described as your "happiest moments, ecstatic moments, moments of rapture." From this research he asserted that "the evidence from the peak-experience permits us to talk about the essential . . . the most fundamental religious experience as a totally private and personal one which can hardly be shared . . . As a consequence, all the paraphernalia of organized religion are to the 'peaker' secondary, peripheral . . . Perhaps they may even be harmful . . . Each person has his own private religion."

This "peak-experience" is what some call "mystical experience" and it is often seen as the heart of the world's religions, common to them all. Furthermore, such mystical experience is seen through the lens of modern psychology. To complete this universally true spirituality, many people add the moral golden rule: "Do unto others as you would have them do unto you," a rule common to most religions. Adding all this together, we end up with the following working definition: in the modern view, true spirituality is psychological well-being combined with the moral golden rule. Doctrine, ritual, and community life are optional extras.

Now let me state clearly that psychology is a valuable science and that I support the golden rule. So in many respects there is nothing wrong with modern spirituality. It deals with many aspects of life previously only dealt with by religion and is a new way of viewing life, different from a religious view.

To look at some of this in practice, I visited the "Pilgrims Mind Body Spirit" web site and found there an astonishing range of mystical possibilities, combined with the full range of New Age practices such as tarot, crystals, and feng shui. A striking dimension here is the emphasis on healing, both physical and psychological. Taking an edition of the site's online magazine at random, I found articles entitled: "There's Life After Depression," "Improving Self-Esteem," and "Healing and Meditation Sanctuary." Nobody could possibly argue with the value of the aims described in those titles and there is much good advice there. So, for example, the article on self-esteem deals with how to make sure that you think good thoughts about yourself, which is helpful; to this, however, religion would add the love of God as a vital source of self-esteem, together with humility, as a source of true knowledge of one's self. The major religions of the world provide a bigger picture that can reveal hidden aspects of human nature while at the same time revealing the divine that is beyond our experience. Within this wider context people have a better chance of discerning the real nature of their needs beyond the demanding clamor of immediate desires.

◆——— SO WHAT IS RELIGION? ———◆

People commonly contrast "spirituality" with "organized religion." I do not think they are seriously suggesting that any kind of organization renders spirituality invalid. So I prefer to talk about "classic religion" as a better way of describing the world's most common religious traditions.

The simplest way to understand classic religion is to begin by reflecting on human desires. From your own experience you will know that the human heart is always set on something: each of us is devoted to something; there is always some shrine (or indeed shrines) at which a person worships. There is usually no single object of human desire and people worship many gods; their hearts are torn in many, sometimes contradictory, directions. Looked at in this way, everybody is religious: all human beings spontaneously worship idols, whether they acknowledge the fact or not. This is seen in expressions such as: "Money is his god," or "Her fans worship the ground she walks on." Such objects of desire are the idols or gods in people's lives, and the god upon which the human heart is most commonly set is the self; as somebody once said of a wealthy entrepreneur, "He is a self-made man who worships his creator." That description could fit most of us, not just wealthy entrepreneurs.

If everybody is religious in this sense, not everybody is spiritual, using "spiritual" in the early, Pauline sense. That is to say, not everybody has noticed their idolatry and so their devotion is self-centered rather than rooted in the Spirit of God. In some modern spirituality movements this tendency is affirmed rather than challenged. The interior world is enthroned as god and its desires are paramount; each individual is responsible for their own spiritual progress and decides how to pursue it. Truth is personal.

Classic religion is about being set free from the idolatry of people, objects, and techniques. It is about being set free from the constantly shifting sands of human desire. In classic religion you do not pick and choose; you learn a whole way of life. Religion offers us an educative process that helps us to see the whole of life in a different way. That is effectively what happened to Tony in the final episode of *The Monastery*. His life was reframed and he stepped away from his own desires; he arrived not only at faith but also at obedience to God. He now knows that he not only wants to pray but that he also feels under an obligation to pray.

The way that Christian faith invites us to undertake this educative process is not just by persuading us to believe that God exists; as St. James puts it in his epistle, even the devils do that. The creed invites us to say: "I believe *in* God." By the addition of "in" the Christian faith invites us to make God the object of our desire and of our worship. This same emphasis is found in Islam and Judaism. These three religions all share the same first commandment: "I am the Lord your God, you shall have no false gods before me." And in their differing ways, the religions of Asia also invite people to recognize their unworthy desires and to turn to a wider horizon, toward the divine. The trouble is that modern society makes such an arrogant self-assessment of its own worth that it cannot accept that it has any false gods or that it needs to look beyond its own boundaries. Modern society says of itself: "We are a self-made society and we worship our creator."

Classic religion is quite simply a broader and richer reality than that offered by many modern spiritual movements such as the one advocated by Maslow. For example, the notion of peak or rapture is just one small part of classic religion, and yet Maslow asserted it to be the center of his new religion. Or the idea that true spirituality is private: this is very narrowing compared to the classic view that religion is a communal event lived out through public rituals and human relationships, as described in the chapter on community (Step 5). Finally, any classic religion has specific doctrines about God or the gods, but the modern approach disdains doctrine and is content with, as William James put it, "whatever they (the individuals) may consider the divine." This view excludes the capacity of religious doctrine to expand hearts and minds, to lead people into areas that they have never experienced or considered, to save human beings from the smallness of their private lives.

◆——    SPIRITUALITY SHOPPER    ——◆

By concentrating on the inner world and making spirituality all about that inner world, the modern spirituality movements have been accused of dulling our society's
awareness of economic justice, of political rights, and of
social inequality. After the political upheavals of the 1960s
people have turned inward and now see psychological self-
improvement as the key to their future well-being. Karl
Marx famously observed: "Religion is the opium of the
people." Yet recently, two contemporary Marxist critics,
Jeremy Carrette and Richard King, adapted Marx's famous
slogan and said that nowadays, "Spirituality is the opium
of the people." They went on to add a further reflection on
the current function of religion in society. Religion, they
said, was the repository of "the richest examples we have of
humanity's collective effort to make sense of life." For them,
where modern spirituality is short-sighted and accommo-
dating, religion is prophetic and challenging.

Yet modern spirituality often looks like classic religion.
It achieves this by taking elements from the classic religions
and recasting them in a new context. A prime example is
the Barefoot Doctor series. Let the cover of a recent book
in the series, *Liberation* (2002), speak for itself: "As always,
Barefoot Doctor offers the full prescription: Taoist healing
methods, with an added pinch of Hinduism, Buddhism,
Shamanism, Humanism, and with a heavy smattering of

timeless Basic Commonsensism . . . the perfect antidote to depression, deprivation, fear, loneliness, grief, grudges . . ." This series aims to answer all your personal development needs from a range of resources drawn from many religions (except noticeably Christianity!). Such elements are no longer seen as stepping stones toward the God who can set us free from idolatry; rather, they have become marketable slices, ready to meet the needs of the consumer.

This tendency to take religious elements and reuse them for consumerist ends was well illustrated by a television program called "Spirituality Shopper." The program can best be described as having offered, metaphorically, a spiritual supermarket, with notional aisles labeled "Buddhism," "Christianity," "Judaism," etc. This really was "pick-and-mix" spirituality. A twenty-nine-year-old woman advertising executive was offered a range of spiritual activities and invited to choose what she fancied. So she was introduced to Buddhist meditation, a Jewish Sabbath Eve meal, and some Christian Lenten charity. Her final choice was whirling dervish dancing. But the very title gives away the problem with this approach: shopping for religion is now making even religion part of the consumerist ideology.

The spirituality shopper builds those parts of religion that make them feel good into their own "spiritual" path, so that it becomes another antidote to the consumer/producer treadmill alongside their holidays and their hobbies. So, amazingly, our journey through modern spirituality has brought us back to the very beginning of this book. Instead of saving us from the treadmill, we find that much modern spirituality is in fact part of it.

A good feature of modern spirituality, however, is that it leads people to learn about the religions of the world. Learning about them is fruitful, as it opens up the bigger picture of life's meaning. But at some point, one has to choose either a whole religion or no religion. Constructing one's own spirituality is a possible outcome of this learning, but it does not deal with the fundamental challenge of the wayward desires of the heart. Only obedience to God can do that. The religious learner cannot escape the need for a wholesale commitment at some point; otherwise they stay at the level of religious shopper. This is the danger that I highlighted in the discussions that Nick and I had with each other in *The Monastery*. Nick is an Anglican by upbringing and a serious student of Buddhism; but on his own admission he was sitting on the fence about ultimate commitment. His experience at Worth and his subsequent retreat for a month with the Carthusians have helped him to arrive at a deeper Christian faith.

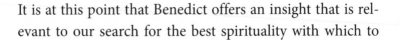

## THE BEST OF MODERN SPIRITUALITY

It is at this point that Benedict offers an insight that is relevant to our search for the best spirituality with which to furnish our sanctuary. Chapter 1 of the Rule is entitled "The Kinds of Monks," and Benedict wants to make clear that not all monks are of equal merit. There is one kind of monk that he finds "detestable"—namely, those "who with no experience to guide them . . . have a character as soft as lead" and are "still loyal to the world by their actions." He continues: "Their law is what they like to do, whatever strikes their fancy. Anything they believe in and choose they call holy; anything they dislike they consider forbidden" (RB, 1:8b–9). That is a fair description of many people today who claim to be "spiritual" and is a strong condemnation of "spiritual shopping." For Benedict, the spiritual shoppers are missing the heart of real spiritual living. He concludes chapter 1 by saying of them: "Let us pass them by, then, and with the help of the Lord, proceed to draw up a plan for the strong kind" (RB, 1:12–13). And the strong kind are those who opt for one, stable path.

There are parallels between the ways in which spirituality went astray in Benedict's day and the way it goes astray today. Spirituality strays when it is self-regarding and self-referential, taking as its point of reference "whatever strikes [one's] fancy." Such furnishings will be out of place in the sanctuary we have been building. Yet there is a positive side to many of the aspects of modern spirituality that I have highlighted: the positive side is evident when these trends occur within a framework of obedience and community. In the context of religious life today, as part of a classic religious commitment, they have much to offer. While the desires of the human heart are wayward, when purified by the discipline of classic religion, they are the voice of God speaking in us. I will examine this further within a Catholic context because that is one I can speak about personally, but many other Christian churches would affirm the same view.

There is much to be learned from the impulses of contemporary spirituality. Although often resisted at first, many modern insights have been absorbed into the church. The questioning of classic religion throughout the modern era has helped religious practice to develop new ways of enabling people to be religious. At its best, classic religion is now a humbler affair, open to dialogue and development.

The Catholic Church has no higher authority than a Council of the Church during which the Pope and all the bishops meet together to proclaim the faith. The last time this happened was in the 1960s at the Second Vatican Council. That council issued a statement about what God reveals and stated: "God has revealed humanity to humanity itself." This deceptively simple statement means that Christian faith offers a vision of being fully human, which involves all aspects of life, not just peak moments or times in church. Many modern sciences are of inestimable value in revealing the nature of humanity, but they are not dealing with the connectedness of life's many parts nor do they offer a vision of purpose. Unity and purpose are divine qualities, given to us by God—qualities that people increasingly seek through the individual experience offered by modern spirituality.

Human experience is now understood by the church as the stuff of Catholic spirituality: my relationships and my work, my hopes and my fears, the highs and the lows. Flowing from this there is a greater awareness that my social context affects my spirituality: if I have had an abusive father, saying the prayer "Our Father" is a real difficulty and I need to find a way through that; if I am a disabled person, I will have distinctive and valuable insights. Abigail Witchalls, for example—the young Catholic mother who was stabbed as she walked with her child and is now paralyzed—blinked out the following haiku to her father a few weeks after she was attacked:

*Still silent body*
*But within my spirit sings*
*Dancing in love-light.*

Such insight and beauty from the experience of its members form an increasingly rich part of the Catholic Church's life.

Another modern emphasis is on the importance of the individual; in the church this has led to a realization of the wide variety of ways in which God works. There is no one way to pray and no single path of growth. The gospel remains constant, but there is now an appreciation of the different ways to God that flow from it. Children, native peoples, those living in poverty—all are now able to express their Christian faith in diverse ways. It has been my privilege to preside at Mass for children here in England, and at Mass for the poorest shanty-dwellers of Lima. Within the set framework of the Mass, each can express their individual insight: the simple prayer of intercession of a child finds expression, as does the anguished cry of the poor man who dumped soil at the foot of the altar saying it contained the blood, sweat, and tears of his people. Expressions such as these, of the individual voices of the participants, generate real worship.

## CONCLUSION

So having found some good furnishing from among the modern offerings, our sanctuary is now complete. But we must now face a final truth: even within this marvellous sanctuary and its furnishing, we are going to die. Rather than face death, modernity wants to delay it or at least control it, because death appears to confirm that life is hopeless. Our final step is to ask: is life—even life in the sanctuary—finally hopeless?

## Further steps toward spirituality

*On the web:* www.anamchara.com is a beautiful site that lists books and web sites introducing all aspects of Christian mysticism.

*In a book: The Cloister Walk* by Kathleen Norris is the story of how living alongside Benedictine monks for eighteen months reshaped her spirituality.

# STEP 7:
# Hope

*As we progress in this way of life and in faith, we shall run on the path of God's commandments, our hearts overflowing with the inexpressible delight of love.*

Rule of St. Benedict, Prologue

It has been my privilege to see many of my monastic brethren die well. After a full life they have accepted death serenely; sometimes pain and discomfort made this very difficult, but that could not detract from their readiness to accept death when it came. The ability to die well is a seriously underrated skill in western society; having watched it close up, I believe that it is one of the most encouraging things you can ever witness. Yes it is sad to lose a brother and we rightly mourn their loss, but in their dying well they leave us a great parting gift.

Part of the problem is that western society has removed death from the world of the family to the world of medicine; this has greatly reduced the suffering of the dying person but has left the living with minimal contact with the dying process. This has now extended to the rituals after death as well. Some people think that children should not be taken to funerals, and modern funeral rites are often brief, impersonal affairs at a crematorium. A time of mourning has disappeared as a practice for most people and is considered by many to be a gloomy, Victorian custom. The Victorians famously exaggerated death and kept sex out of sight, but the reverse seems to be true in our day.

Death is inherently frightening, but the marginalization of death adds to that fear. By contrast, Benedict wants the monastery to be a place where death is not marginalized and he tells his monks: "Day by day, remind yourself that you are going to die" (RB, 4:47). This may seem a morbid suggestion but it is in fact the opposite. Benedict wants his monks to remember their mortality so that they might live with a sense of the urgency and goodness of life now: in the Prologue to the Rule, Benedict urges his monks to "run while you have the light of life, that the darkness of death may not overtake you" (RB, Prologue:13). The thought of death adds a sense of immediacy to life itself; we must run because life is short. Benedict also sees continuity between life and death because the whole purpose of the monastery is to foster constant awareness of the presence of God. In life this is difficult, but in death we will have the blessing of knowing the presence of God continuously in heaven. "Faithfully observing God's teaching in the monastery until death, we shall through patience share in the sufferings of Christ that we may also deserve to share in his kingdom" (RB, Prologue:50). The monastic life requires a stripping away of the inessential to enable us to be constantly aware of God. Death is the ultimate stripping away and the ultimate encounter with God.

I want to illustrate this by recounting the remarkable story of seven monks, known as the Atlas Martyrs, who died together in 1996. Their story involves not only the spirituality of death but also the politics of terrorism, which caused their death. Their story is a sign of hope in a world that despairs when confronted by death and terrorism.

The Abbey of Our Lady of the Atlas lies in a small village called Tibhirine, about sixty miles south of Algiers, and it has been on this site since 1937, when a community of French Trappist monks settled there. In the early 1990s they found themselves caught in a vicious civil war between the military government and the GIA, an armed group who wanted to end all western influence in the Islamic state that they hoped to establish. In 1993 the GIA issued an ultimatum that all foreigners must leave the country by December 1st under pain of death.

There were few Christians left in Algeria, but these monks chose to stay. They stayed out of love for Algeria and especially out of love for their Muslim neighbors, with whom they had excellent relations; the villagers were also being terrorized and saw the presence of the monks as a reassurance. In the absence of a village mosque, the villagers had the use of a room in the monastery for prayer, and the monks and villagers together ran a market garden.

On Christmas Eve 1993 an armed GIA group penetrated the monastery, and the leader demanded that the monks and the Prior, Father Christian, compromise themselves by helping the GIA. Father Christian refused his demands and the leader said: "You have no choice," to which Father Christian replied: "Yes, we have a choice." Father Christian knew that recently this man had killed fourteen Croatian construction workers who had lived nearby and that he was renowned for his cruelty. Father Christian informed him that the presence of guns in the monastery was not allowed and that the arrival of the group had interrupted the monks as they were about to celebrate the birth of the Prince of Peace. Surprisingly, the leader apologized and the gunmen withdrew, but said they would return.

The monks now knew that there was an immediate danger of death at the hands of these gunmen. After agreeing that three should leave, nine remained. These monks now had to struggle with constant fear, and it was at this time that Father Christian wrote a letter or testament to be opened in the event of his death. Throughout 1994 and 1995 several members of Catholic religious orders were murdered by the GIA, yet the monks continued in their regular monastic life. During these two years the monks' life was characterized by a deepening sense of communion—of *koinonia*. There were inevitably tensions between them, but they remained focused on the task of building communion—communion with each other, with God, and with their Muslim neighbors. In a letter to Father Christian another monk described their task: "that in our day to day relations, we should openly be on the side of love, forgiveness and communion, against hate, vengeance and violence." By having death daily before their eyes, their lives took on a new energy of love. They really were running while they had the light of life, knowing that each day the darkness of death might overtake them.

Then, one night in March 1996, gunmen arrived and abducted Father Christian and six other monks. A month later an ultimatum was issued to the Algerian government: free all GIA prisoners or the monks would have their throats slit. In May that threat was carried out, and the seven Atlas Martyrs joined the growing number of Christians who had given their lives out of love for their Muslim neighbors.

The testament of Father Christian was now opened and its beginning reads as follows:

*When we face an adieu . . .*
*If it should happen one day—and it could be today—*
*that I become a victim of the terrorism which now*
*seems ready to engulf all the foreigners living in Algeria,*
*I would like my community, my Church and my family*
*to remember that my life was GIVEN to God and to*
*this country.*

Father Christian had come to see that his death was a moment of gift, one that required great mindfulness and great purity of heart—two qualities that the monastic life had fostered in him to a remarkable degree. This purity of heart even extended to his assassin, of whom he writes at the end of the letter:

*And also you, my last-minute friend, who will not have*
*known what you were doing: yes, I want this thank you*
*and this adieu to be for you too, because in God's face*
*I see yours. May we meet again as happy thieves in*
*Paradise, if it please God, the Father of us both.*
*Amen! Inch Allah!*

For Father Christian, death was the supreme moment of love. His example and that of the other monks offer us hope when confronting not only death but also that most frightening of all modern developments, terrorism. They were sustained by their faith in the risen Christ who overcomes death, and this faith strengthened their communion to an extraordinary degree. The contrast with the modern attitude to death could not be clearer. For the modern person so busy in self-absorbed activity, death is the final, hopeless denial of everything that has filled life. For the Atlas Martyrs, death was the final expression of the faith, hope, and love that had filled their lives.

So let's now consider the implications of this story for finding sanctuary. What I believe the Atlas Martyrs bring to the sanctuary from the monastic tradition is the need for an altar to be built there. An altar is a place for making offerings to God and even for offering life itself to God. In return, God blesses the one who makes the offering, and this reciprocal process is called sacrifice. The origin of "sacrifice" is the Latin *sacrum facere*—"to make holy." So as you offer your life on the altar, God blesses you and makes you holy. During those two years of waiting for their death, the monks offered themselves in communion each day: in return, God blessed them and made them holy, ready to die as martyrs.

On a less dramatic scale, when anybody finds sanctuary they will also find an altar of sacrifice. None of us lives or dies for our own sake; finding sanctuary is also finding out what God is asking of us. It is about asking for God's blessing and living out the vocation that he will give us in return, a vocation to love others in a way that is unique to each of us. So at the heart of the sanctuary we build an altar in order to give and receive the sacrifice of love, which is at the heart of true religion.

At the beginning of our search for sanctuary I welcomed in particular those whose attitude to religion is: "I don't know." I hope that this book is helping you to build a secure sanctuary, but it will come as no surprise to you that I, a monk, consider religion to be a vital part of that sanctuary. So I want to conclude by dispelling some modern misrepresentations of religion and then affirming the vital role of religion in the twenty-first century—not just the role of religious *elements,* but the role of a whole religion.

The story of the Atlas Martyrs stands in its own right as a testament to hope; but I would like to look more widely at some of the issues that it raises about the role of religion as a *source* of hope.

◆——— RELIGION CAUSES PEACE ———◆

This subtitle is purposely provocative because the phrase we most commonly hear is its opposite—namely, religion causes war. In the story of the Atlas Martyrs we see religion apparently promoting both war on the part of the terrorists and peace on the part of the monks. Like all human

capabilities, religion can be abused, but it is my belief that in the everyday life of the modern world religion has a vital role to play in promoting peace. Many readers will find this last sentence hard to believe so, once again, let's turn to modern research to shed some light on this difficult issue.

In February 2004 BBC Television broadcast a program entitled "What the World Thinks of God." As part of their research they commissioned Bradford University's Peace Studies Department to carry out an audit of wars over the last hundred years, with specific reference to the role of religion in causing those wars. Looking back at history, they analyzed the actual mechanisms by which religion might cause war and found several possible ways in which this occurs. These mechanisms might be the promise of salvation to those who fought the infidel, or the intention of religious leaders to seize holy places—both key factors in the medieval crusades. Or they might be the desire to convert the enemy, as in the wars of the Reformation.

The researchers then analyzed the thirty-two wars of the twentieth century. Their conclusions were that only three had a significant religious element. They considered the Israeli–Arab wars, for example, to be wars of nationalism and liberation of territory (and I would add that the same is true of the Irish wars and conflicts). They noted that the current campaign being waged by Arab terror groups is largely about political order in the Arab countries, especially the presence of foreigners there. These groups use the language of religion, but the use of religious language to justify terrorism is disowned by mainstream religious leaders.

Political leaders use differences in confessional faith as a way of mobilizing support for political wars, and it is mainly in this way that religion becomes a factor in war. Furthermore, the main wars of the century (the two world wars, the Russian civil war leading to Stalin's regime, the Chinese civil war leading to Mao's regime) claimed 75 percent of all casualties of war in the twentieth century; they killed 150 million people. None of them is attributable to religion. The recent conflicts in which religion has played a significant role have killed only 1 percent of the number of victims of secular wars.

This study provides evidence that religion is not a major reason for war in modern times. But the two great moments of violent religious conflict in Europe, the Crusades and the Reformation, have cast a long shadow over the popular mind, so that even though there have been no truly religious wars for many centuries, even intelligent commentators still insist that religion causes wars. The reality, however, is that in the modern world it is governments, and not religions, that cause wars.

Looking beyond the statistics of war to religious teaching, the main religious traditions have little truck with war or violence. All advocate peace as the norm and see genuine spirituality as involving a disavowal of violence. Most religious traditions regard war as a failure to achieve genuine spirituality and impose special constraints on the conduct of war when it does occur.

If religion is only rarely a cause of war nowadays, the next question is: how might religion cause peace? The Catholic Church defines peace as "not simply the absence of war; it is the fruit of justice." A peaceful society is a just society. Thus, providing adequate resources for education, housing, and health care is a vital way in which people build peace; but while these physical resources are a necessary part of peace, they are not sufficient. To build peace there is also a need for spiritual resources, and religion can provide these in a unique way. The key spiritual resource that religion offers is hope. "The future of humanity," the Church stated at the Second Vatican Council, "lies in the hands of those able to pass on to future generations reasons for living and hoping." Reasons for living and hoping are the heart of true religion and the greatest gift that religion gives to humanity. Terrorism is fed by despair and war is sustained by fear. Religion offers hope against despair and love that casts out fear. That is exactly what the Atlas Martyrs offered to the people of Algeria: while the men of violence used the language of religion to promote terror and hatred, the monks offered the reality of religion to promote reasons for living and hoping.

## ◆——  A RELIGIOUS SANCTUARY  ——◆

Religion is the cement that pervades the whole sanctuary to hold together all the constituent parts. The cement of religion makes sure that the sanctuary is reliable and won't fall down in a gale. Religion protects the sanctuary from theft, when everybody from salesman to terrorist is trying to steal sections of the building and palm them off as the whole to those outside who are desperate for some religious or spiritual shelter. I believe that the world's great classic religions can fulfill this task of sustaining true sanctuary in the twenty-first century in new and creative ways. To do this, people will need to leave behind that dull, twentieth-century, liberal view that all religions are the same; anybody with any imagination can see that this is simply not true. The alternative is not mutual condemnation and aggression, however. The alternative is exemplified by the work of the late Pope John Paul II, with his groundbreaking initiatives in reaching out to the leaders of the world's religions. The fruitfulness of this work was borne out by the unprecedented number of non-Christian religious leaders who attended his funeral. He was the first Pope to visit a mosque and the first to visit a synagogue. For the World Day of Prayer held in Assisi in 1986 he invited leaders of all the world's religions to spend a day together in prayer, and in so doing these leaders witnessed powerfully to peace as a core value in religion. His words on that day are an agenda for the role of religion in the twenty-first century.

First, he insisted that this coming together of leaders of different churches and religions did not imply "any intention of seeking a religious consensus among ourselves or of negotiating our faith convictions." Nor was it a concession to relativism in religious beliefs, because "every human being must sincerely follow his or her upright conscience with the intention of seeking and obeying the truth." He showed that you can have deep faith in your own religion and have friendship with other religions, without any need to water your faith down to some gray lowest common denominator.

He then went on to state that the aim of the day was peace. "Without in any way denying the need for the many human resources which maintain and strengthen peace, we are here because we are sure that, above and beyond all such measures, we need prayer—intense, humble and trusting prayer—if the world is finally to become a place of true and permanent peace."

Intense, humble, and trusting prayer in the cause of true and permanent peace: this is a good summary of where our quest for sanctuary has led us. So many people say that they want true and permanent peace in their personal lives and for the world, but saying that you want it is not enough. The desire for peace has to become your burning ambition, your first priority and not just something that you express at Christmas. This book has tried to show how to translate that desire into action through the demanding work of finding sanctuary. This final step invites you to participate in a classic religion as part of that work. The modern prediction that religion will die out has proved untrue, and a key task in the twenty-first century is for people to engage thoughtfully with their religious tradition and, from that base, to work with other religions to build peace.

Benedict describes his monastery as a "school of the Lord's service." This means that one of his most basic insights is that you need to be in some kind of school if you are to live out the way of peace; you can find tranquillity in private but you cannot find peace there. In Benedict's day, as for his monks and nuns today, the only possible schools of peace were the monastery and the wider church. In our global society, we can recognize, as did Pope John Paul, that all the world's classic religions can be schools of peace for those who follow them in good conscience. So I want to suggest that finding sanctuary requires that you freely choose to place yourself in the context of the church or of some other classic religion. You may eventually want to join that church or religion, but you should certainly ask for its wisdom and guidance if you are to make real spiritual progress.

A classic religion is a place where you will avoid the tendency to be self-absorbed that characterizes so much current western spirituality; you will instead be doing what the Pope describes as "seeking and obeying the truth." A classic religion will help you to take all the steps described in this book: it will offer you grounding in silence, schooling in prayer, a community to teach you obedience, and a living experience of humility. It will help you to absorb the best of modern spirituality and ignore the rest. Finally, it will lead you on to hope—hope in this life and in the next.

## FINDING SANCTUARY IN GOD

In the end, we find sanctuary in God; he is our natural sanctuary. At the beginning of our search I said that if your response to matters of religious faith was "I don't know," then you should just keep an open heart and mind as you read. Now, at the end of the book, you will find the parable of the prodigal son presented as an example of *lectio divina*. In this parable the younger son found his way back to his father but the elder son could not bring himself to participate in that joyful homecoming. You too may still hang back and be reluctant to join in the celebration of faith; but you nonetheless have a place in the story, a place where the father urges but does not condemn.

I hope, however, that you now feel able to join the prodigal son on the journey home to your God-given sanctuary—a journey in which we advance by going back to the God who made us. On that journey back to our natural sanctuary, Benedict is a sure but demanding guide as to what steps we should take and, as always, he wants us not to dawdle but to run! "As we progress in this way of life and in faith, we shall run on the path of God's commandments, our hearts overflowing with the inexpressible delight of love" (RB, Prologue:49).

To encourage you on the way, I offer a final story from the desert fathers and mothers. A young monk once went to see his superior: "Father," he said, "I must leave the monastery because I clearly do not have a vocation to be a monk." When the older monk asked why, the younger monk replied: "In spite of daily resolutions to be good-tempered, chaste and sober, I keep on sinning. So I feel I am not suited to the monastic life." The older monk looked at him with love and said: "Brother, the monastic life is this: I rise up and I fall down, I rise up and I fall down, I rise up and I fall down." The young monk stayed and persevered.

*Further steps toward hope*

*On the web:* www.findingsanctuary.org is a site designed to sustain the task begun in this book. There are resources from the great religions of the world so that you might grow in faith and understand better the religions of other people.

*In a book: Crossing the Threshold of Hope,* in which the late Pope John Paul II answers questions posed by a journalist, including questions about Christian faith and the religions of the world.

# Lectio Divina:
# The Prodigal Son

I invite you to join me in some shared *lectio divina,* taking as our text one of the great parables of Jesus, the parable of the Prodigal Son. The story is found in the fifteenth chapter of Luke's gospel, verses 11 to 32, and after each short section, I will offer you some of the echoes that this text raises in my soul as I read it.

---

There was a man who had two sons. The younger one said to his father, "Father, give me my share of the estate." So he divided his property between them. Not long after that, the younger son got together all he had, set off for a distant country and there squandered his wealth in wild living.

---

Why does a son leave his home? Perhaps he is bored with the routine and feels he needs to "take a break." So he leaves his busy life at home and seeks out the supposedly good times. But the promise of good times turns out to be an illusion.

Have I run away from God the Father?

Why do I run away?

Do I persuade myself that I'm having a good time away from Him?

*Lord, help me not to run away from you and from life.*

---

After he had spent everything, there was a severe famine in that whole country, and he began to be in need. So he went and hired himself out to a citizen of that country, who sent him to his fields to feed pigs. He longed to fill his stomach with the pods that the pigs were eating, but no one gave him anything. When he came to his senses, he said, "How many of my father's hired men have food to spare, and here I am starving to death!"

---

The son feels real hunger in his stomach but he feels more than hunger for food. He is lonely and nobody cares about him. He is desperate.

Have I ever felt real despair?

Where do I turn when I feel desperate?

Do I feel hungry and empty, even when I have plenty?

*My God, my God, why have you forsaken me?*

---

I will set out and go back to my father and say to him: "Father, I have sinned against heaven and against you. I am no longer worthy to be called your son; make me like one of your hired men." So he got up and went to his father.

---

In the moment of weakness, he turns back to father. But this is also the moment of enlightenment because he believes that his father will not reject him.

Am I capable of being this humble?

How can I learn this humility?

Where do I find such strong faith that God accepts me?

*Lord, help me to come back to you.*

_____

But while he was still a long way off, his father saw him and was filled with compassion for him; he ran to his son, threw his arms around him and kissed him. The son said to him, "Father, I have sinned against heaven and against you. I am no longer worthy to be called your son." But the father said to his servants, "Quick! Bring the best robe and put it on him. Put a ring on his finger and sandals on his feet. Bring the fattened calf and kill it. Let's have a feast and celebrate. For this son of mine was dead and is alive again; he was lost and is found." So they began to celebrate.

_____

While he was still a long way off, the father forgave him. Such a small step by the son meets such strong love from the father. The father never stopped loving him but now he can show that love. What joy to picture God wanting to show his love if only I will turn to him.

Can I admit that I am a sinner?

What is blocking that admission?

Do I rejoice in forgiveness?

*Lord, have mercy on me a sinner.*

Meanwhile, the older son was in the field. When he came near the house, he heard music and dancing. So he called one of the servants and asked him what was going on. "Your brother has come," he replied, "and your father has killed the fattened calf because he has him back safe and sound." The older brother became angry and refused to go in. So his father went out and pleaded with him. But he answered his father, "Look! All these years I've been slaving for you and never disobeyed your orders. Yet you never gave me even a young goat so I could celebrate with my friends. But when this son of yours who has squandered your property with prostitutes comes home, you kill the fattened calf for him!" "My son," the father said, "you are always with me, and everything I have is yours. But we had to celebrate and be glad, because this brother of yours was dead and is alive again; he was lost and is found."

The elder brother is a busy and serious man. Of course he is angry but sadly, he is unable to step outside his own world and his own self-importance. What a missed opportunity.

Where is the elder son in me? Am I too busy and self-important?

Do I feel jealous of others?

Why can't I just let go?

*Lord, make me a channel of your peace.*

As a conclusion, say a familiar prayer such as the "Our Father."

# Acknowledgements

My first sanctuary was my family. I thank them for that gift, and single out in particular my mother for continuing to be such a timeless sanctuary, and my eldest brother Tony, who has given typically generous help at both the beginning and the end of the writing process.

My present sanctuary is Worth Abbey and this book is dedicated to my monastic brethren there. In particular I thank Fathers Luke Jolly, Mark Barrett, and Martin McGee for offering helpful critiques of the text.

I thank my editor, Helen Garnons-Williams, who had the idea for the book and who has offered unstinting support at every stage of writing. It was a pleasure to work with such a perceptive and generous editor.

The value of the monastic way in everyday life was brought home to me by *The Monastery,* and I want to thank the Tiger Aspect production team for the sensitive way in which they portrayed our life: especially the Series Producer Gabe Solomon, the Executive Producers John Blake, and Charles Brand, the Producer/Director Dollan Cannell, together with Elizabeth Stopford, the Assistant Producer and Hettie Hope, the Program Manager. I also thank Jacqui Hughes, the commissioning editor at the BBC, for believing in the project. It has been a privilege to work with people who combine media skill with integrity. And alongside them I must thank the five men listed at the start of the book; their honest search is the heart of the program, and it is a delight for us monks to count them among our friends. A final thanks to the thousands of people who wrote to us and visited us following the broadcasts. Your affirmation is very dear to us, and a great encouragement as we continue to build up the sanctuary that is Worth Abbey.

In the *lectio divina* on "The Prodigal Son" I have used the New International Version of the Bible, and I also acknowledge my debt to the Manquehue Movement, an inspiring group of Chilean laypeople who live out the Rule of St. Benedict with a special emphasis on *lectio divina*.

I gratefully acknowledge permission from Peter Dwyer to reproduce extracts from the 1980 translation of the Rule of St. Benedict, published by Benedictine colleagues at Liturgical Press, Collegeville, Minnesota. Their scholarship is an invaluable asset in approaching the Rule.

# Bibliography

The works listed below are highly recommended for further reading and have been particularly useful in the writing of this book.

Boyle, N., *Who Are We Now? Christian Humanism and the Global Market from Hegel to Heaney* (Continuum International Publishing Group, 1998)

Carrette, J. and King, R., *Selling Spirituality: the Silent Takeover of Religion* (Routledge, 2005)

Casey, M., *Truthful Living: St. Benedict's Teaching on Humility* (Gracewing, 2001)

Collins, J., *From Good to Great* (Random House Business Books, 2001)

De Mare, P., Piper, R. and Thompson, S., *Koinonia: From Hate, through Dialogue, to Culture in the Large Group* (Karnac Books, 1991)

De Waal, E., *Seeking God: the Way of Benedict* (Canterbury Press, 1991)

Foster, D., *Reading with God: Lectio Divina* (Continuum Publishing, 2005)

Illich, I., *In the Vineyard of the Text* (University of Chicago Press, 1993)

Lash, N., *The Beginning and the End of Religion* (CUP, 1996)

Merton, T., *New Seeds of Contemplation* (Continuum Publishing, 2003)

Norris, K., *The Cloister Walk* (Riverhead Books, 1997)

Pope John Paul II, *Crossing the Threshold of Hope* (Jonathan Cape, 1994)

Stewart, C., *Prayer and Community* (Orbis Books, 1999)

Ward, B., *The Desert Fathers: Sayings of the Early Christian Monks* (Penguin Classics, 2004)

Williams, R., *Silence and Honeycakes: the Wisdom of the Desert* (Lion Hudson, 2004)